LET THE READER UNDERSTAND

Sean Goan

# Let the Reader Understand

## THE SUNDAY READINGS OF YEAR A

the columba press

First published in 2007 by
the columba press
55A Spruce Avenue, Stillorgan Industrial Park,
Blackrock, Co Dublin


Cover by Bill Bolger
Origination by The Columba Press
Printed in Ireland by ColourBooks Ltd, Dublin

ISBN 978 1 85607 590 9

# Table of Contents

# Introduction

*Reading the Old Testament*

As the title suggests, this book is intended to help the reader understand what is being read as we gather every Sunday to celebrate the Eucharist. Even though Catholics have been encouraged to read the scriptures since the Second Vatican Council many find it difficult to break with a four hundred year old tradition that warned against reading them! So we find ourselves today in this unusual position of showing our reverence for the scriptures by staying away from them. Happily, however, the situation is changing and many more Catholics are discovering that the Bible is a very nourishing source of life, helping them to develop their relationship with God and to deepen their appreciation of the great riches of their own tradition. Even so, it is not uncommon to hear people say things like: 'I don't like the God of the Old Testament, he is very angry and judgemental. I prefer to read the gospels; they are much easier to understand.' The problem with this is that it fails to appreciate the fact that all the writers of the New Testament were Jewish and totally steeped in the writings and traditions of the Jewish people that are contained in the Old Testament. Not only that, but Jesus himself loved to read the scriptures of his people and quoted them often.

As with most things in life, a little understanding goes a long way so the purpose of this introduction is to offer some background information about how the Old Testament came into existence, about the books it contains and why they are important for Christians. Since this is a short introduction it will be very limited in its scope but it will be helpful to people who have never studied theology or scripture before.

*How did the Old Testament come about?*

The Old Testament is the name given by Christians to the collection of books found in the first section of their Bible. Nowadays it is sometimes referred to as the Hebrew Bible, reflecting the fact that this collection of writings makes up the sacred text of the Jews and was, for the most part, written in Hebrew. It is thought by some that calling it the Old Testament is disrespectful to Jews as it implies the New Testament must be somehow superior. However, with no disrespect to the Jews to whom we are totally indebted for these great books, I will continue to refer to it as the Old Testament. There are a couple of reasons for this. Firstly, as we shall discover later, the books of the Christian Old Testament are not exactly the same as the Hebrew Bible; secondly they are presented in a different sequence. Moreover I don't go along with the idea that the word 'old' is offensive – that smacks of ageism to me!

It is important to note that the Bible, as we have it, resulted from a long period of history during which the oral and written traditions of the people of Israel were handed on from generation to generation. For most of this period there is no Old Testament as we know it. The written traditions were finally edited and brought together in the period after the exile of the Jews in Babylonia (500-450 BC) when the Pentateuch (or Torah) became the central text of the Jewish people. These are the first five books of the Bible and are of great importance because they pass on a record of the faith experience of the Israelites over many centuries. It must be stressed that the books of the Old Testament are not primarily history books but rather are a record of the people's experience of God with them expressed in a variety of ways including poetry, myth, epic, story, law code and folk tale. To fully understand any book of the Bible it is necessary to try and enter into the world of its authors and the people to whom it was addressed. This involves having some awareness of their history, culture and literary traditions. Recognising that the Bible came about as a result of a long process is helpful when we are confronted with difficult texts or stories which appear cruel or unjust. We must try to put them into their overall context and remember that within the Bible there is an ongoing development in the people's understanding of God.

Since the Old Testament begins with the Book of Genesis and the story of Creation, we might think that this reflects the order in which the books were written, but that is not the case. For the Israelites it is the experience of the exodus that is the key to who and what they are as the People of God. This experience provides the cornerstone for their covenant relationship with God and its influence is to be felt throughout the Old Testament. While the Torah or Pentateuch was being edited and becoming established as the sacred text of the people, work on other books began. The writings of the prophets, the so-called historical books and the other writings about wisdom and the prayers of Israel were also edited and copied. Gradually these books were associated together as the sacred texts of the Jews, so that by the time of Jesus they had become a vital part of the Jewish faith. This is evident from the fact that a couple of hundred years earlier they had been translated into Greek for those Jews who were living away from the Holy Land and who did not know Hebrew. It is also clear that by the time of Jesus these books were being read in the synagogue during Sabbath worship. The books were revered because they showed how God had revealed himself to his chosen people. An awareness of the process that gave rise to the Old Testament helps us realise that the Bible did not drop ready-made from heaven as the Word of God. It would be more accurate to say that it came from the ground up. As people of faith we believe that this process was inspired by God but it still took place through all the ups and downs of human history and it would be fair to say that most of the people involved did not know they were writing the 'word of God'.

*What is in the Old Testament?*
If you look at the table of contents of a Bible you will see that the Old Testament is divided into four sections. They are the Pentateuch, The Historical Books, The Wisdom Books and the Prophets. This arrangement is somewhat different from the Hebrew Bible where there are just three sections. The Prophets and the Historical books are combined into one and come second while the third section is called 'The 'Writings' and comes last. The Christian ordering of the books reflects their interest in seeing the prophets as a kind of bridge to the New Testament since it is in them that the messianic prophecies are to be found and these were of great importance for the early church as it sought to understand all that had taken place in the life death and resurrection of Christ.

## The Pentateuch

This name comes from Greek and means five scrolls and these are the books that make up the Torah or Law of Moses. They are: Genesis, Exodus, Leviticus, Numbers and Deuteronomy. The content covers the story of creation and the spread of sin, the call of Abraham and his descendants, the slavery of the Israelites in Egypt, their liberation and the covenant with Yahweh on Mount Sinai, including the giving of the Law and finally the journey in the wilderness up to the point when they are about to enter the Promised Land. While the final form of the Pentateuch was completed by around 400BC it contains some of the oldest traditions in the Bible. It is believed that the final editors were priests from the Jerusalem temple and their work reflected their concerns around helping the Jewish people to be clear about their identity as God's chosen ones, the importance of worship in the Temple, and fidelity to the covenant.

## The Historical Books

The history traced in these books goes from the entry into the Promised Land under the leadership of Joshua to the time when Nehemiah and Ezra help the rebuilding of the Temple in Jerusalem and the reorganisation of Jewish life after the exile in Babylonia. That is a span of some eight hundred years, but again it is worth saying that this is not history in the modern sense of that word. The books from Joshua to the second Book of Kings tell the story from one point of view. That is, they reflect the theological concerns of the authors of the Book of Deuteronomy whose main interest was in preserving the Sinai covenant. The Books of Chronicles cover much of the same period but with a different slant. Their interest is in the Temple and the promise to David that his descendants should rule. In their different ways the writers stress God's faithfulness on the one hand and the infidelity of his people on the other. Some Bibles will contain other books in this section, namely Tobit, Judith and the Books of Maccabees. These are known as 'deuterocanonical 'or 'apocryphal'. They were part of the Greek translation of the Jewish scriptures that was made in the third century BC. They circulated in Greek or were even written in Greek but were not preserved in Hebrew and so they were left out of the final form of the

Hebrew Bible. The early church preserved these books through the Greek translation and they are accepted as inspired scripture in the Catholic Church.

## The Wisdom Books

This very general title is somewhat misleading as these books vary a great deal in their themes and content. However, the term wisdom is used because it reminds us that there was within Israel a way of thinking about God that was outside the language of the priests or the prophets. Some people were learning from the wisdom traditions of other countries and reflecting on life experience and the wonder of creation. They also grappled with the big questions such as the meaning of suffering. The books in this collection touch on some or all of these themes. They are Job, Psalms, Proverbs, Ecclesiastes, and The Song of Songs. In an addition you may also find two more deutero-canonical books, namely The Book of Wisdom and Ecclesiasticus. The Psalms, which are the prayers of Ancient Israel, still feature very strongly in our worship and are present in the liturgy of Sundays and weekdays.

## The Prophets

The prophets played a very important role in Israel as they felt called by God to speak his word to the people. They came from a variety of backgrounds and were most active during a period between 800 and 450BC. Their preaching was often focused on the covenant, reminding the people – especially their priests and kings – of their obligations towards it especially in relation to the poor and oppressed. However, they also emphasised the faithfulness of God and constantly urged their contemporaries to repent and discover again the loving kindness of their God. As Christians we often associate prophecy with prediction but it needs to be stressed that the prophets were not particularly concerned with predicting future events. When they spoke about what was to come is was with a view to showing how God's faithfulness would endure. They also looked to a time when a descendant of King David would rule on the throne. This person would be God's 'anointed one' (Messiah in Hebrew) and their writings on this topic became very important for the early church as it came to see Jesus as the fulfilment of the scriptures. In the collection there are four major prophets and twelve minor ones. Isaiah, Jeremiah, Ezekiel and Daniel are the major ones and these are names with which many people are familiar.

*Why do we read the Old Testament at Mass?*
The simple answer is that we read it for the same reason we read the New Testament and that is because we believe that it is the inspired word of God. In other words, we read it because we wish to know what God is revealing to us. You might argue that since Jesus is the Word of God then wouldn't it be enough to read about him in the gospels and discover there all we need to know. This point was made very forcefully in the second century AD when a certain Christian called Marcion thought that the Old Testament gave a bad impression of God, and so he advocated that the Bible should be made up of only the gospel of Luke and some of Paul's letters. Thankfully our Christian ancestors recognised that this was a baby and bathwater solution and they insisted that the Christian Bible must contain both Testaments because they speak about the unfolding of the one plan of the one God to make known to the whole world the salvation offered through Jesus. Saint Jerome, who was one of the greatest scripture scholars of the early church, put it like this: 'Ignorance of the scriptures is ignorance of Christ.' In other words, if we have little or no knowledge of his Bible how can we understand Jesus who used it so much and his first followers who read it with fervour so that they could come to a deeper knowledge of him? We can see this process at work in the story of the Road to Emmaus as told in Luke 24. Two disciples of Jesus are sad and downcast as they leave Jerusalem after the death of Jesus. They encounter a stranger on the road who uses the scriptures to help them see their situation in a completely new way and leaves their 'hearts burning within them' as they come to understand who Jesus is through a reflection on the Old Testament.

There is another reason for reading the Old Testament at Mass and that is because it contains some of the most comforting, challenging and inspiring writing about God that can be found anywhere. The Psalms teach us about praying as we are with a whole range of emotions. The Prophets shake us up to think differently about what God wants and the relationship be-tween faith and life. The enormous variety of images and metaphors remind us again and again that we should not con-tent ourselves with just one perspective on who God is and where he might be found but rather we must allow God to force our minds and hearts open to see the divine mystery at work in a whole host of ways. All of this presumes that we are not reading the Bible literally and that we recognise that the Old Testament is the word of God in human words. Therefore we approach it within the tradition of faith, asking the Spirit who inspired its writing to also inspire our reading so that we might pray with the Prophet Jeremiah: 'When I found your words, I devoured them; they became my joy and the happiness of my heart.' (Jer 15:16)

# The Season of Advent

*First Reading: Isaiah 2:1-5*

The first reading is from Isaiah and indeed will continue to be not only for the rest of Advent but also for Christmas day. The reason for this is that Isaiah's prophecies are characterised by hope and a wonderful, universal vision of God's will to save all people. Even though this prophet lived and preached between 740 and 687BC, during periods of great crisis when the kingdom of Judah and Jerusalem itself were under threat of destruction from Assyrian empire, he remained utterly convinced of the faithfulness of God and he encouraged the people to do the same. In this reading he sees a great future for his beloved Jerusalem and this will be God's doing. Instead of foreign armies coming to destroy, the nations will come for instruction to hear the word of God and to learn his ways. In a beautiful and now famous image, the prophet sees people abandoning the ways of conflict in order to pursue the path of peace. Weapons of war are forged into agricultural implements as Israel, along with the other nations, learns to benefits from the earth's goodness and walk in God's light.

*Second Reading: Romans 13:11-14*

The second reading touches on a theme that is central to the season of Advent and that is that, while we may look back to the first coming of Christ to derive comfort and encouragement from its message, we must never forget that central to the proclamation of the gospel is the belief that Jesus is to come again. This is important because accepting a second coming ought to determine how we live our lives today. St Paul thought that this second coming would not be in the far distant future and so, when writing to Christian communities, he urged the faithful to conduct themselves as people who know what the future holds. They must give up the decadent lifestyle which was so prevalent in the world around them and let their lives become focused on Christ.

*Gospel: Matthew 24:37-44*

There is certainly no sign of Christmas in this reading, taken from near the end of Matthew's gospel. Here Jesus is presented as giving his last sermon to his disciples before the events of Holy Week. The theme of his preaching is the idea that the Messiah will come again and people will be held accountable for their actions. Therefore the disciples are called upon to be always vigilant and aware that accepting Jesus is not just a once off decision but a constant striving to live the way he wants us to. This is an important theme in the gospel of Matthew where there is an insistence on the need for faith to express itself in a genuine attempt to do God's will in our lives. What that means is shown by Jesus who throughout his public life lived as 'God with us', a name given to him at the time of his birth (Matthew 1:23). Here is the connection with Advent. This season begins with a reflection on the future and where we are heading. It is an appeal for repentance, a true change of heart that will allow us to recognise how and where God is at work and to respond to him in the challenges of every day.

*Reflection*

In our consumer-driven world, preparations for Christmas began a couple of months ago and for many the last four weeks leading up to this feast are a time of frantic activity and increasing stress. These readings for the first Sunday of Advent are an invitation to us to rediscover the essentials. At the heart of this season is the word of God with its message of hope and its challenge to all believers to stand back from the demands the world imposes on them in order to let the light of Christ show them the way. That is the only way we can celebrate Christmas as followers of Jesus and come to appreciate its true meaning.

## THE SECOND SUNDAY OF ADVENT

*First Reading: Isaiah 11:1-10*

In this text the prophet, who has had close contact with several kings of Judah during his lifetime and who often found them wanting, looks to a new future when a king would arise from the dynasty of David (Jesse was David's father). This future king would rule by the Spirit of God and is depicted as the ideal just ruler who possesses the gifts required of someone fit to govern the chosen people of God. The Spirit gives him wisdom and insight, he has knowledge of the Lord and this implies an intimate friendship as well as the fear of the Lord. This latter gift might be better translated as a reverence for God as it refers to having a right understanding of who we are in relation to the Creator. His reign is characterised by the attributes associated with the covenant which bound God to the people and the people to God and these are faithfulness and integrity. The prophet then envisions the perfect harmony which would follow on from this complete adherence to the covenant. Even the conflicts which are part of the natural world cease as God's will for the world is realised: 'They do no hurt, no harm on all my holy mountain.' All this is possible because the country is filled with the knowledge of the Lord. Isaiah's dream moved generations of Israelites to pray for such a time and such a ruler. Their longing for a messiah (God's anointed) came to pass not in the palaces of the kingdom but in the simplicity of Bethlehem. Jesus, filled with the Spirit, shows us the true face of God, and makes possible a friendship with God which goes beyond Isaiah's wildest dreams. He calls us to create the harmonious kingdom with him.

*Second Reading: Romans 15:4-9*
Following the pattern of all the letters, Paul draws his epistle to a close urging the communities to live out the practical consequences of their faith in Christ. The Letter to the Romans is the longest of Paul's writings in the New Testament and in it he offers profound insights into the mystery of Christ's life and our union with him through baptism. With these verses we have the apostle's advice to the community on their life together. The community in Rome had both Gentile and Jewish Christians in it, so Paul encourages them to reflect upon God's mercy towards everyone. They must recognise that what unites them is Christ's friendship with each of them. Just as he has shown tolerance and understanding, so too must they.

*Gospel: Matthew 3:1-12*
The figure of John the Baptist looms large in the season of

Advent and that is because in the gospels he is depicted as the one preparing the way for the long awaited Messiah. He does this in a very stark and uncompromising way in the extract we read today. The call to repentance is couched in the language of apocalyptic, that is a worldview which believed that God would come soon to judge the world. John recognises that this event is indeed coming soon in the person of Jesus but what he does not know yet is just how God will reveal himself in Jesus. It will not be in an apocalyptic catastrophe but in the remarkable preaching of the kingdom of God, in deeds of healing and compassion and in parables of forgiveness and growth. While John's call for repentance may have been based upon the fear of impending judgement, he is right in insisting that repentance is the only way to prepare for the future God is offering us.

*Reflection*
The authentic response to Jesus is indeed the kind of transforming repentance or change of heart that John is asking for. The prophet's hope for a new world might seem like an impossible dream but, considering the great event of Christmas when heaven and earth are joined in the birth of God's Son, we come to understand that indeed nothing is impossible to God. We also see that since we have been loved so much by God then we too should seek to love one another and that is the only repentance worth talking about.

THE THIRD SUNDAY OF ADVENT

*First Reading: Isaiah 35: 1-6, 10*
The prophet Isaiah was so influential in his own lifetime that subsequent generations collected his sayings and prophecies and when, at a later stage, the people experienced the turmoil of war and exile, another (unnamed) prophet took up Isaiah's themes of hope and the fidelity of God and preached a similar message. In chapter 35 we have some of his writing and it is among the most beautiful and inspirational in the entire Bible. He sees God bringing back the exiles, and the entire creation rejoicing with all those who are making their way home through the wilderness. There is a transformation here which turns

desert into fertile land and heals a wounded people. All this is God's work and the faithful respond by shouting out for joy. Now the blind see, the deaf hear and the lame walk; sorrow and lament are ended as a new day is dawns. The reference to vengeance is to be understood in the context of the person who undoes the harm done to a family member. God as a Father to Israel is bound by his covenant love to care for them and that is the reason for his action in today's reading.

### Second Reading: James 5:7-10

The focus of this reading is the advent theme of expectant waiting. Its author is thought to have been James who was also known as the brother of the Lord (Acts 12:17) and was the leader of the church in Jerusalem. In the early church there was some disappointment that the promised return of Jesus had not taken place and indeed some were losing heart. Towards the end of his letter, James encourages them to be patient and uses examples from nature and from the scriptures. The farmer must be patient and let nature take its course as he awaits the harvest. So too in their own tradition the prophets had to be patient as they submitted to the word of God. Similarly Christians must learn patience as they await the revelation of Christ.

### Gospel: Matthew 11:2-11

We can understand why John sent messengers to Jesus to ask about his identity if we remember last week's gospel when John was preaching about God's impending judgement. When Jesus comes preaching the kingdom he does so not with the threat of hellfire but with the offer of unconditional forgiveness and healing for all who would receive it. Hence John's question: could this really be the one? Jesus answers by referring to the message of Isaiah in today's first reading, a vision of the healing power of God restoring a broken and weary people to life. However, Jesus realises that some, even those as holy as John, may be scandalised by the idea. What Jesus is talking about goes way beyond anything John would have imagined and that, in a sense, is what makes him least in the kingdom of God, where the last will be first and the greatest will be the servant of all.

*Reflection*

This is a very apt message as we continue our preparation for Christmas. Familiarity breeds contempt so they say and whatever our grasp of the meaning of Christmas it fails to do justice to its deepest meaning. It is only with the eyes of faith that we can glimpse the kind of transformation Isaiah spoke about in the first reading. We are invited to have the courage to see God in love with the world and we are invited to live fully in the world without fear because we know that God will never give up on us. Let us pray for a renewed faith this Advent and Christmas so that the wonder and joy of this great feast do not pass us by.

THE FOURTH SUNDAY OF ADVENT

*First Reading: Isaiah 7:10-14*

This short reading from the early chapters of Isaiah refers to a time in the history of Jerusalem when king Ahaz is attempting to hold on to his throne by means of military alliances. Fearful for his own future, he is seeking the backing of Assyria against his nearest neighbours but the prophet Isaiah is warning him not to choose this path but rather to trust in God. Ahaz pretends to be humble and says he will not ask God for a sign. However, the prophet sees through him and says God will give him a sign whether he wants it or not. The sign is that a child will be born who will be a better king than he is. In its own time, this was thought to refer to King Hezekiah who followed Ahaz and who was a more faithful ruler. Much later, however, St Matthew saw in this text a reference to the birth of Jesus, who is called Emmanuel, a name which means 'God-is-with-us' (Matt 1:21). For Matthew this reading was given even more power as he took it from the Greek translation of the Old Testament where it states that 'a virgin will conceive and bear a son'. This is the gospel for today's Mass and we now understand in a way that Isaiah and Ahaz never could have the significance of the title Emmanuel. In Jesus, God is joined to the human race as the 'word made flesh' and this is a union which gives an unsurpassable dignity to every human being.

*Second Reading: Romans 1:1-7*

In these opening verses of the letter, Paul introduces himself to the church in Rome where he is unknown. In his other letters, he is writing to communities that he has already visited or even founded. In this case, however, he is preparing the way for a visit he hopes to make and wants to let them know the gospel he is preaching in other parts of the empire. As always his message is totally focused on the person of Jesus because he wishes everyone to understand the power of the resurrection and the transformation it brings to our relationship with God and with one another. Later in the year we will be returning to the letter to the Romans for a more continuous reading which will give us an opportunity to study its powerful teaching. For the moment it is enough for us to notice how Paul begins by emphasising both the divine and human in Jesus. He is the Son of God and the descendant of David and it is he alone who can bring us 'grace and peace'.

*Gospel: Matthew 1:18-24*

Matthew's account of the birth of Jesus differs in several ways from the version of St Luke which places a great stress on the role of Mary and her 'yes' to God. For Matthew the emphasis will be on Jesus as the one who fulfils the scriptures of the Jewish people. This is important for him because his gospel was written for Jews who had become followers of Jesus but who were coming under pressure to abandon their faith. One of the ways Matthew will try to persuade them is to show how Jesus is indeed the one spoken about in the prophecies. He will also use Old Testament figures and images to connect the story of Jesus with the story of the people of Israel. Hence the importance of Joseph who is like Joseph in the Book of Genesis who was also guided by dreams and was faithful to God.

The unique circumstances of the birth of Jesus are shown through the prophecy from Isaiah. In the person of Jesus, God is truly with us and, as Matthew says at the end of his gospel, will stay with us until the end of time.

*Reflection*

Now the four weeks of Advent are coming to their climax as the feast of Christmas draws near. The Sunday readings have invited us to prepare by challenging us to admit our need of God and to really repent, not just of our petty sins but of our smallness of mind and heart that constantly restricts our ideas of God and his infinite love. In a spirit of prayer and openness, we are now ready to pray with great hope and fervour: 'O come, o come Emmanuel.'

# The Feast of Christmas
*(The Readings for the Masses of Christmas are the same for each year of the liturgical cycle)*

## THE VIGIL MASS

*First Reading: Isaiah 62:1-5*
The original setting for this reading was the return of the Jewish exiles from Babylon. The whole experience of war and deportation had been a painful reminder to the people of their failure to live according to the ways of the covenant, but now God speaks to them again about the desire of his heart which is that they should come to know their true worth and how much their God longs to be one with them, just like a bridegroom longs for his bride. The sending of God's son is the ultimate proof that God wants us to know our true worth.

*Second Reading: Acts 13:16-17, 22-25*
In this reading we read a section of a speech given by Paul during his first missionary journey. The town of Antioch in Pisidia was situated in what is now South West Turkey and, as was customary for Paul when he came to a town, he preached first in the synagogue to the local Jewish population. Appropriately for today, he preaches that Jesus is indeed the fulfilment of the long awaited promise made by God that a son of David would be their Messiah and Saviour.

*Gospel: Matthew 1:1-25*
It is suggested that the short form of this gospel may be used, namely verses 18-25. The reason is clear enough as these tell Matthew's account of how Jesus was born to Mary and Joseph in Bethlehem. Matthew emphasises that Jesus is the fulfilment of the scriptures, especially the important verse in Isaiah 7:14. He explains that the child will be called Jesus (Hebrew *Joshua*) because this name means God saves, but in the quotation we are given another name 'emmanuel' – God is with us. The two are fitting for Jesus because one describes what he does and the other who he is. The earlier part of the reading giving the genealogy of Jesus is Matthew's way of affirming that the God who

guided the people of Israel through all their troubled history is active in the birth of Jesus. Just as some of Jesus' ancestors were born in unusual or even scandalous circumstances, so too Jesus comes in an unexpected way.

MIDNIGHT MASS

*First Reading: Isaiah 9:1-7*
The historical setting for this passage is towards the end of the reign of king Ahaz of Judah. The people have been through years of warfare and bloodshed and the threat of invasion by Assyria remains. Into this situation comes the king's son Hezekiah and the prophet Isaiah sees in him a brighter future in which the oppression of recent years ceases and the people can look forward to a time of peace and justice. While the reign of king Hezekiah was an improvement on what went before, it still proved to be a disappointment and so in later years the prophet's words came to be seen as a reference to an ideal king. The early church saw in this text a prophecy about Jesus, the son of David who revealed himself as Mighty God and Prince of Peace. The people who have walked in darkness are all those who have waited for God's intervention in the history of the world and now they can rejoice because on this holy night a 'child is born for us'. The imagery is rooted in the change that is brought about when war ends and a new day dawns and so it captures perfectly the longing that still exists for a time when all people can live in peace, and that is surely the heart of our prayer at Christmas.

*Second reading: Titus 2:11-14*
Titus, who was charged with the care of the church in Crete, had been a fellow worker with Paul and in this letter he is encouraged to be faithful to his task and to preserve the community from the false teaching which would distort the message of the gospel. These verses are appropriate for today because they remind us that even at Christmas it is the work of Christ as risen Saviour that we recall and the stress is on our response to him. Welcoming the child born in a stable means more than mere sentiment. Our lives must change as we continue to hope for his return among us.

*Gospel: Luke 2:1-14*
Luke puts his account of the birth of Jesus in the context of the rule of the emperor Augustus. He is the ruler of the world and the one credited with bringing peace to the empire, yet now in the humblest of circumstances a child is born whose rule will never end and whose power derives not from military might nor economic wealth. He is the true Saviour whose birth is a cause of joy in heaven and on earth and is first announced to the disenfranchised.

## THE DAWN MASS

*First Reading: Isaiah 62:11-12*
This short reading taken from the near the end of the Book of the Prophet Isaiah returns to a favourite theme of the prophet: the faithfulness of God who more than anything wants to save his people from all that would keep them from knowing that they are indeed his beloved children. The daughter of Zion is a reference to the people of Jerusalem, the city of God that for to long has suffered the consequences of war and violence. New names are given here to symbolise the true identity of God's chosen people.

*Second Reading: Titus 3:4-7*
Again in this reading the Christmas message is presented to us in terms of whole story of the good news. God's gift of his Son and the pouring out of his Holy Spirit are based solely on the compassion of the Father. The birth of Jesus is the setting in motion of this one great act of God by which we might come to know our true worth. This is why Christmas is such a wonderful feast.

*Gospel: Luke 2:15-20*
This is a continuation of the gospel used at midnight Mass and tells how the shepherds went immediately to Bethlehem. There they find things as the angels had told them. The gospel offers two responses to the unfolding story. One is that of Mary who 'treasured all these things and pondered them in her heart' and the other is that of the shepherds who went away glorifying and

praising God. As people of faith participating in this feast, we are invited to do the same. Christmas is a time for praise and thanksgiving to God but it is also an invitation to reflect deeply on the mystery that is being put before us.

## MASS DURING THE DAY

*First Reading: Isaiah 52:7-10*
Once again the writings of Isaiah are called upon to bring out the meaning of Christmas and this time we are presented with a message of salvation aimed at the war-weary citizens of Jerusalem. After the failure of so many human kings to guide them in the way of peace, now, at last, God himself their warrior king is coming to console his people and to rule over them.

*Second Reading: Hebrews 1:1-6*
The opening verses of the Letter to the Hebrews sum up in a very simple yet profound way how the early church viewed the coming of Christ. While the prophets of old spoke in a powerful way about the saving will of God and his faithfulness, they never imagined how that will would be finally accomplished and that faithfulness displayed. This is the amazing truth that has been revealed in the person of Jesus who is 'the radiant light of God's glory' and who is therefore greater than any angel or prophet.

*Gospel: John 1:1-18*
The Gospel of John has no account of the birth of Jesus, rather the evangelist chooses to begin his story with a poem and that is the gospel for this Mass. Rather than considering the life of Jesus from the time of his birth, John seeks to find and explore his identity by meditating on Jesus as the Word made Flesh. The Jews to whom the good news was first preached were very familiar with the idea of the word of God through their oral and written traditions. For generations God had made himself and his saving will known to them through his word and now that word becomes human, and as a human being reveals the glory of God in a way that is beyond our wildest imaginings. This is a staggering claim and one that many then, and indeed still today,

find too hard to believe. Yet it is the very heart of the Christmas message.

*Reflection*

There is a remarkable variety in the twelve readings that are given for the Christmas Masses. One of the most striking things about them is that only three of them actually tell the Christmas story. The other nine are taken from both Old and New Testaments and in different ways invite reflection on the feast that is being celebrated. They all challenge us to move beyond the sentiment of the nativity play and to make our own this remarkable truth that we dare not believe. By the 'flesh taking' of God's eternal Word, everybody and everything is made sacred and if we accept this then we must live differently in the world for it really is a beautiful and a holy place and all the cruelty and injustice that surround us cannot be allowed to erase that.

## THE FEAST OF THE HOLY FAMILY

*First Reading: Ecclesiasticus 3:2-6, 12-14*

Ecclesiasticus represents the later stage of the development of the tradition of wisdom literature in the Bible. This book, written about two hundred years before the birth of Jesus, has the usual traits of wisdom writing such as advice on the key to living a good life. Here, in keeping with the feast we are celebrating, the stress is on the relationship between parents and children. The biblical commandment of honouring parents is upheld though there is more about the role of the father as he was considered the head of the house. The tone of this advice is both sensitive and compassionate, as children are urged to care for their parents in their old age. There is also evidence of the Old Testament belief that if you do good you will live a long life: 'Long life comes to him who honours his father.' Such a view was challenged elsewhere, especially in the book of Job and, of course, in the New Testament the life of Jesus shows that this is an oversimplified view. Even though the reason for doing it may be different, the exhortation to live a good life remains valid and forms the basis for a harmonious family.

*Second Reading: Colossians 3:12-21*

Here again we have Paul drawing out the consequences of living the Christian faith as he encourages the church at Colossae to keep Christ and his example at the centre of their lives. He lays special stress on the importance of forgiveness: since God in Jesus has forgiven them, then they must forgive one another. Their life as a community must also be characterised by prayer, with special place given to thanksgiving. What he advises for the larger community is also true for the family units within that community and so he gives particular advice to them. As in the first reading, it was taken for granted that the man was the head of the house and so Paul writes accordingly. If he were writing today, Paul would no doubt express the husband and wife relationship in more egalitarian terms and in so doing would point yet again to Jesus as our example, for he came not to be served but to serve.

*Gospel: Matthew 2:13-15, 19-23*

In this extract from Matthew which brings to an end the infancy story in the gospel, the evangelist shows how God protects and cares for his chosen one. It is useful to remember when reading about the birth of Jesus that all these stories were first told in the light of Easter faith. In other words, in the entire narrative of the life, death and resurrection of Jesus, God is seen as faithful to his promises and to Jesus his chosen one.

The Holy family of Nazareth experienced the pain and anxiety of living through politically unstable times. Herod's son Archelaus was even more of a tyrant than his father and after just a few years was removed from office by the Romans. The incident in today's gospel shows this young family as refugees fleeing violence, and migrants looking for work. Their lot is a common one in today's world.

*Reflection*

Today's feast and the readings put before us are a reminder that families play a vital role in determining what kind of people we become. An atmosphere of love and respect, of acceptance and forgiveness is one that allows us to come to a deeper appreciation of who God is. The readings are also a reminder not only of our duty of care towards one another but also of the fact that no matter how difficult and uncertain our circumstances, God is always at work to bring good out of evil.

SECOND SUNDAY AFTER CHRISTMAS

*First Reading: Ecclesiasticus 24:1-2, 8-12*
As on the Feast of the Holy Family we once again find ourselves reading from Ecclesiasticus which is also sometimes known by the Hebrew name of its author, Sirach. This is one of the latest books of the Old Testament, being written around 190BC and Sirach, as well as being very familiar with the traditions of his own people, was also aware of the influence of Greek philosophy on the Jews of his time. For this reason he sought to present the faith of Israel in a way which showed that it was superior to the arguments of their pagan neighbours. The extracts in today's reading come from the climax of the book in chapter 24 where we find a poem in praise of the wisdom of God. Earlier in the Old Testament the idea of wisdom is personified (Proverbs 8) and described as a woman who was God's instrument at the moment of creation. Sirach then develops this idea and says that later on wisdom was directed by God to come and live on earth. This wisdom was then to be found in Israel and its holy book the Torah (the Law of Moses). It is clear that for the evangelist John this notion of God's wisdom pitching its tent on earth allowed him to see Jesus as the Word (or wisdom) of God made flesh who lived among us (literally 'who pitched his tent among us').

*Second Reading: Ephesians 1:3-6, 15-18*
Unlike the other letters of Paul, there is no reference in Ephesians to the specific problems of a local Christian community or church and so it is thought that this letter may have been intended as a circular to be read as widely as possible in the early church. The opening verses are a hymn of praise in which the apostle's enthusiasm for all that God has done for us in Jesus spills over into a wonderful prayer of blessing. We are encouraged to recognise that through Christ we have been blessed with every spiritual blessing in the heavens. In other words, in giving us his own son God has held back nothing in his desire that we should

live through love in his presence. After praising God, Paul then turns to praying for all who follow Jesus and he asks that they be given the wisdom to understand just what it is that they have entered into and in this prayer too Paul's excitement at what it means to be a Christian is once again very evident.

*Gospel: John 1:1-18*
This is the text used for the Christmas day Mass (see above).

*Reflection*
With these readings we are reminded again just how profoundly beautiful the Season of Christmas is. All human life is given a dignity which, if we take time to reflect upon it, transforms our understanding of ourselves and the world in which we live. The light breaks through into our fragile human hearts and shows us what is possible if we only have the courage to believe in what God has done and continues to do for us through his Son the Word made Flesh. The evangelist who penned the gospel for today did not come to the insight he shares with us on his first encounter with Jesus, nor even immediately after the resurrection. Rather these words are the fruit of many years of prayer and reflection on the mystery of the person of Christ. As such they are a reminder to us we too must engage with this mystery through prayer and reflection if we really want to make our own the gift that God gives us in the person of his Son.

# The Season of Lent

*First Reading: Genesis 2:7, 3:1-7*

In the Season of Lent the readings prepare us to celebrate the resurrection of Jesus at Easter. This is done by taking us on a journey of faith through the Old Testament, highlighting both our turning away from God and God's efforts to bring us back. So it is appropriate for today's first reading that we should start with a story of the beginning of our alienation from God. The significant opening of this reading is the image of God breathing a breath of life into the man. We live therefore by the breath of God, which in Hebrew, the language of the Old Testament, can also mean the Spirit of God. However, the story shows that this life-giving relationship is soon threatened by our unwillingness to accept that we are indeed creatures and that there are things which are beyond us.

In the story, the serpent is the cunning beast who suggests the disobedience but it is only in much later tradition that this figure becomes identified with the devil. Adam and Eve's action has immediate consequences; they realise they are naked and they become ashamed. The situation of harmony with self, others and God is destroyed. The rest of the Bible could be summed up as the story of God's efforts to undo the harm of sin and to restore us to himself, a work that is finally accomplished through the events of Easter.

The modern reader must bear in mind that the creation accounts in Genesis are not scientific or historical accounts of what took place at the beginning. These inspired stories are God's way of revealing the truth about himself and our relationship to him.

*Second Reading: Romans 5:12-19*

During Lent, unlike the rest of the year, there are sometimes clear connections between the first and second readings and this is clearly so today. The Letter to the Romans, Paul's longest and most theologically advanced epistle, was written around 57AD before his visit to the Christian community in Rome. He wrote it

because he was making his way to Rome and he wanted to intro-
duce the community there to his ideas about Christ and the
gospel, since he had neither founded the community there nor
had ever visited them. In today's section of the letter he is explaining the wonders of what Christ has done by comparing
Christ to Adam. His point is simple: Adam the first man sinned
and we all suffer the consequences of his action for we too are
sinners. But now through Jesus, the new Adam, we are all restored to friendship with God. He uses legal language to drive
the point home. As a result of Adam's disobedience in which we
all share we have been tried and found guilty, but now, as a result of Christ's obedience, we have been acquitted.

For Paul the imagery of life and death provides a key to understanding what Jesus has done. Death is not merely the end of
life – it is being cut off from relationship with God and so it can
apply to us even when we are alive. Life, on the other hand, is
friendship and union with God and that is now possible because
through Jesus God has once again made us alive to him.

*Gospel: Matthew 4:1-11*
The gospel for the First Sunday of Lent is always that of the
temptation of Jesus in the wilderness. After his baptism in the
Jordan, Jesus was revealed as God's son and now he is to be put
to the test in the same way as the Israelites had been tested in the
desert. Like them, Jesus is tempted to reject God in three ways.
Firstly, he is urged to turn stones into bread and so satisfy his
hunger. Jesus rejects the temptation with an appeal to scripture.
Human beings need more than bread to really live; they need to
be nourished by the word of God. In the second temptation the
devil suggests that Jesus put God to the test to see if he will pro-
tect him and this time it is the devil who quotes scripture. Jesus
rejects the idea because it would show a lack of trust. Finally the
ultimate test is to offer Jesus the world's kingdoms in return for
worshipping the devil. In the Old Testament idolatry was
Israel's greatest failure. They repeatedly abandoned the true
God to go after empty promises of power and wealth, a way that
seemed more rewarding than fidelity to the covenant with its
concern for justice and the plight of the widow and orphan.
Jesus dismisses the devil with a reminder of the scriptural com-

mand to worship God alone. In this gospel Jesus shows us the way to be the true children of God.

*Reflection*
As we begin another Lent we might find it hard to relate to the dramatic struggle told for us in the gospel or the strange narration about a serpent in the Garden of Eden. Our experience of temptation is probably more mundane. They are the daily temptations not to bother, or to simply go with the crowd. We are tempted to believe that what we do is not going to make any difference anyway. However, the end result is the same, God is squeezed out of our lives and in living only for ourselves we become miserable. Lent is an opportunity to rediscover the joy and freedom there is in living for others as Christ did. So let's begin this season by inviting him to show us how to do that and how to both recognise and then reject the voice of the tempter.

THE SECOND SUNDAY OF LENT

*First Reading: Genesis 12:1-4*
This brief reading marks the beginning of the second stage in the history of our salvation. The first eleven chapters of Genesis tell the story of creation and the spread of sin, but now with the story of Abraham we begin the faith journey that commences with one family who in turn become the People of Israel, God's chosen ones who in their turn prepare the way for the new People of God, the church throughout the world.

This stage of salvation history will be characterised by the faith or faithlessness of those who are called and Abraham will serve as a model for all who follow. In today's reading Abram, as he is first known, is called to leave behind everything with which he is familiar and go to a land that God will show him. With this call comes a promise of blessing and, quite simply, he does as he is asked. Faith in the scriptures is not so much about believing certain truths as trusting oneself totally to the living God.

*Second Reading: 2 Timothy 1:8-10*
Three of Paul's letters were not written to 'churches' as such but

to individual leaders of some of those communities. For this reason they became known as his pastoral epistles as he was giving pastoral advice in them. Two were written to Timothy and one to Titus. Both of these men shared in Paul's missionary work and are mentioned frequently in his other letters and the Acts of the Apostles. Timothy was the son of a mixed marriage between a Jew and a Gentile and as such was a great help to Paul in his efforts to bring Jewish and Gentile Christians together. It is thought that he may have been a leader of the church in Ephesus when this letter was written.

In this reading Paul is urging Timothy to remain faithful as he faces the difficulties that come his way as a result of the good news. He must remember that his is never alone and that he can always rely on the power of God that has brought him to where he is now.

*Gospel: Matthew 17:1-9*
Just as the temptation of Jesus in the wilderness is the gospel for the first Sunday in Lent each year, so the story of the transfiguration is always told on the second Sunday, and this year we have Matthew's version of this remarkable event. It takes place immediately after Jesus has told his disciples for the first time that his ministry will end in rejection and death. He brings Peter, James and John up a mountain where his appearance is dramatically altered. We are told his face shines like the sun and that his clothes become brilliantly white. In biblical terms these changes indicate the presence of heavenly beings (see Daniel 10:6-7) and this is confirmed by the appearance of Moses and Elijah who represent God's revelation through the Law and the Prophets. In the Gospel of Matthew, Jesus is portrayed as the fulfilment of the Law and the Prophets. The next two events confirm yet further Jesus' identity. Firstly a cloud overshadows them. This is a reminder of the time when God's presence among the Israelites was indicated by a cloud covering the Tent of Meeting (Ex 40:34). Then finally the voice of God is heard as it was at the baptism identifying Jesus as his Son but adding the all important words 'Listen to him.' Like the Israelites of old at Mt Sinai, the disciples fall prostrate terrified at this manifestation of God's presence. However, the dramatic events come to a sudden conclusion when Jesus touches them and tells them not to be afraid.

*Reflection*

Today's readings are about the journey of faith and the importance of trusting in and relying on God. Abraham and Paul are both examples of people who leave everything to embark on a journey that would change their lives and the lives of countless others completely. The journey of faith is not an easy one and, in a world that increasingly wants to rely on proofs and certainties, they are examples of what is possible when we put our trust in God. In the story of the transfiguration Jesus is transformed in glory but later in his faith journey he will be transfigured by pain and suffering. In both these events, his identity remains the same and thus he shows us that God is not only found in the high points but also when the road is at its darkest.

THIRD SUNDAY OF LENT

*First Reading: Exodus 17:3-7*

The incident in this story occurs soon after the chosen people have escaped from slavery in Egypt. Even though they have witnessed the power of Yahweh triumphing over the forces of the Pharaoh, the Israelites are slow to believe that their God is capable of bringing them through the wilderness with all its inherent dangers. Returning to a theme that is present from the early chapters of the Book of Exodus, the people turn against Moses and accuse him of being the source of all their difficulties. 'Why did you bring us out of Egypt?' Their God is quickly forgotten in the face of their thirst and once again Moses is forced to intercede on their behalf. God responds to Moses' urgent prayer and, as a reminder of what has already happened, he is told to take the staff which he had earlier used to divide the sea in order to strike the rock from which the water shall flow for the children of Israel to drink. In keeping with a practice found in many biblical stories, the place names associated with these events are explained. The words Massah and Meribah in Hebrew mean 'trial' and 'contention'. The whole story and indeed the theme of Exodus is summed up in the question: 'Is Yahweh with us or not?' And through all the events which are recounted the answer is repeatedly 'YES!'

*Second Reading: Romans 5:1-2, 5-8*

In these verses from Romans we touch on one of the great themes in Paul and that is the idea of justification or being made 'righteous'. In using this language Paul was trying to show what had been achieved by the death and resurrection of Christ. In the previous chapter he had spoken of Abraham's faith and how, by trusting in God, Abraham had been reckoned as being righteous, i.e. a friend of God. Now through our faith in Jesus we too have becomes friends of God, we have, in a certain sense, come into his presence and can look forward to sharing fully in the glory of God. This we know because 'the love of God has been poured into our hearts by the Holy Spirit which we have received'. For Paul, love is the key to understanding what has taken place in Jesus. For there can be no greater proof of God's love for us than the fact that Christ died for us while we still sinners. We had done nothing to earn this love; it is pure gift. That is the staggering claim of Christianity and Paul's grasp of this insight is the driving force behind everything he said and did.

*Gospel: John 4:5-42*

For the next three Sundays the readings from Matthew are set aside and very important and profound texts from the gospel of John are put before us. It is in this way that Catholics are introduced to John's gospel which does not have a year to itself in the liturgical cycle. Over the next three weeks each reading from John will consider the ways in which we may come to a vibrant Easter faith in Jesus, one that satisfies our deepest thirst, (the Samaritan Woman) opens our eyes to really see (the Man Born Blind) and one that brings us to the fullness of life (Lazarus).

This week the story shows how the woman from Samaria comes gradually to an understanding of who Jesus is and how this in turn transforms her life as she commits herself to him in faith and, in the process, becomes the first missionary in the gospel of John. In the gospel these long discourses are not meant to be read as normal conversations but as opportunities to explore who Jesus is and to respond to him. Hence the story relies heavily on symbolism. The important metaphors here are thirst and water. Thirst is expressive of our need for God and water points to the gift of the Spirit that quenches our thirst fully. The encounter with Jesus shows how faith may flourish in the most unpromising of circumstances. As a woman of Samaria it might be reasonably expected that a Jewish teacher would have nothing to do with her. But that is not the way of God, and Jesus reveals that he is driven by a deep desire to do the work his Father gave him, namely to bring everyone to an awareness of their dignity as children of God.

*Reflection*

Sometimes when reading the story of the Exodus we find ourselves wondering how was it that the Israelites were so slow to believe that God was with them after all that they had witnessed. Yet spectacular and all as the dividing of the sea was, can it compare with the events of Good Friday and Easter Sunday? Even so, like our ancestors in the faith, we too can find ourselves asking: 'Is God with us or not?' when the circumstances of our lives are difficult. It is at such times that we do well to focus on the mystery of Easter and the God who gives us living water to drink from a source that will never run dry, and like the Samaritan woman in today's gospel we must ask: 'Lord, give us that water always.'

## THE FOURTH SUNDAY OF LENT

*First Reading: 1 Samuel 16:1, 6-7, 10-13*

On first reading this text you could be forgiven for wondering what has this to do with the themes of Lent, but it is important on two counts. Firstly, it introduces us to the idea of a messiah, and secondly, it reminds us that God is not interested in appearances but in the heart. The dramatic story tells how Samuel was told by God to go to a small town called Bethlehem to the house of Jesse and that among his sons he would find the future king of Israel. Samuel is asked to do this because Saul, who was the first king in Israel, has failed to live up to his calling. These are difficult times for the Israelites as their enemies the Philistines are pressing in on them and they lack the proper leadership to see them through the crisis. It is with this in mind that Samuel views the seven sons of Jesse, but to his surprise God has chosen none of them. So he is forced to ask, is there another? Since David was the youngest and engaged in the menial task of minding the sheep, he hadn't even been considered. Yet to everyone's amazement it is this boy who is called to be king and, we are told, the spirit of God seized on David and remained with him from that day on. The ceremony of anointing is important for out of this comes our word Messiah which means 'the anointed one' in Hebrew. This is a key moment in the history of Israel for in later years, when they look for a messiah, they will look for a descendant of David who will shepherd the chosen people. Jesus, the Son of David, will reveal himself as that true shepherd of Israel.

*The Second Reading: Ephesians 5:8-14*
The letter to the Ephesians is thought to be one of Paul's later writings as it shows differences in style and content from his classic work, the letter to the Romans (written around 57AD). Even though it seems to be addressed to the community at Ephesus (in modern Turkey) it is considered to be a homily meant for the wider church. These verses are taken from the final part of the letter when Paul is usually encouraging his readers to live out the consequences of the teaching he has given them in the epistle. They have a new life now in Christ and must live accordingly, so they are to abandon their former pagan ways which were characterised by what Paul calls 'futile living'. The contrast is really between light and darkness. In choosing Christ and being baptised, they have become like the light and so their lives are to be characterised by complete goodness, right living and truth.

*Gospel: John 9:1-41*
This wonderful extract from the fourth gospel is a masterpiece of storytelling and tells us much about how the evangelist saw the work of Jesus. As with the Samaritan Woman someone who is considered an outcast takes their place among the community of believers. The story also relies heavily on symbolism; this time blindness and sight are contrasted with darkness and light. These images are used to makes us think about what it means to come to faith. We are presented with the difference between the blind man who gradually comes to acknowledge who Jesus is and the Pharisees who become progressively more hard hearted

and are shown to be the only really blind people in the story. The openness of the man born blind, his growing conviction about Jesus and the fact that he suffers for it are all pointers to what is needed in the person who wants to believe. The fact that he is anointed and washed are symbols of baptism and the new life it offers, but Jesus' opponents cannot see this and are unable to move beyond a purely legalistic interpretation of the Law of Moses that would forbid what Jesus has done. It is probably also true to say that the blind man's parents represent those who have some insight into the truth but are afraid to move forward because of the challenges it will pose.

*Reflection*

The origins of the season of Lent go back to the time when new converts to Christianity were preparing for baptism, a sacrament that was originally associated with Easter. The Christian community joined together in celebrating the very reason for its existence by welcoming new members who were receiving the light of Christ for the first time. These new converts were helped in their preparation by Christians who saw that this was also a good time for them to renew their commitment to Christ and his gospel. So the story of the man born blind is very appropriate for it is an invitation to us to acknowledge our blindness, the extent to which we do not see with Christ's eyes and so become shut up in our own little world, closed off from what God wants to give us. So let us ask for the courage to open our eyes in order to be humbled, enlightened and transformed by the vision of God.

THE FIFTH SUNDAY OF LENT

*The First Reading: Ezekiel 37:12-14*

In order to fully appreciate the impact of these verses it would be useful to read from the beginning of chapter 37 of Ezekiel. This prophet was writing at the time when the city of Jerusalem and its temple were destroyed by the Babylonians and many of its inhabitants were carried off into exile (587BC). The prophet, who was a priest in the temple, was one of the exiles and so he feels very deeply the pain of the loss and he understands the crisis of faith which it gave rise to for many Israelites. It is to these people then that the wonderful vision of the dry bones is given. Though they feel they are like skeletons, dried up, without hope or direction, God will bring them to life again. Just as he created a living being by breathing into the nostrils of Adam in Genesis 2 so now in this vision he breathes new life into their weary bones. They appear to have died but God will raise them up from their graves and cause them to live. He will put his spirit (breath) within them and they will really know that God has done this. At the time of writing this prophecy concerned the return from exile which was to take place some fifty years later. At this stage in Israel's history there was no belief in an afterlife or the resurrection and it is only in the light of Easter that these verses take on a whole new depth of meaning.

### Second Reading: Romans 8:8-11

For Paul the Christian is not someone who merely follows a set of commandments given to him by Jesus. If this were the case there would be little or no difference between Judaism and Christianity since devout Jews tried to follow the Law given to Moses on Mt Sinai. The essential difference for Paul is that the disciple of Christ lives the life of the Spirit. Through baptism the very Spirit of God has been given to us and this becomes our driving force. It is this which enables us both to know what God wants and to do it. In these few verses from chapter 8 of Romans Paul is stressing once again that the Christian lives a spiritual life. Unfortunately this language has been taken by some to mean 'otherworldly', referring to a holy person who does not live in the here and now. However, that is not what Paul has in mind. For his great insight is that the same power which raised Jesus from the dead is at work in us to make us alive to God in the ordinary details of our everyday existence. So the unspiritual person is the one who is turned in on himself and away from others and God.

### Gospel: John 11:1-45

Now we come to the last public act of Jesus in the fourth gospel. As with the previous two dramatic stories, a metaphor is presented to us that challenges us to reflect deeply about who Jesus really is and what it is that he brings. He not only satisfies our

thirst for God and allows us to see, in fact he brings us to a completely new life. The woman's thirst, the man's blindness and
Lazarus' mortality are all means by which we are brought to understand that Jesus is indeed 'the resurrection and the life'. The
raising of Lazarus is the culmination of the seven 'signs' that are
worked by Jesus in this gospel. The evangelist deliberately
avoids the term miracle because he wants us to think about what
Jesus' actions tell us about God's will for humanity. In restoring
Lazarus to life Jesus anticipates the meaning of his own death: 'I
have come that you may have life and have it to the full' (Jn
10:10). As the story unfolds we identify with the grief of Martha
and Mary at the death of their brother, and their disappointment
that Jesus, their friend, did not do something to prevent it. In the
midst of their pain, Jesus invites them to see from another perspective but even he is overcome with sorrow and weeps. At
this low point he calls on them all to have the faith that will
allow them to see the glory of God, and God's glory is precisely
what he reveals. Lazarus comes out of the tomb and the story
comes to an end with the significant words: 'Unbind him and let
him go free.' Ironically the raising of Lazarus from the dead is
the reason why Jesus is put to death according to the gospel of
John. He will lay down his life for us and in the mystery of the
resurrection will reveal God's indestructible desire for our salvation.

## Reflection

Today's readings and the gospel which tells of the raising of
Lazarus all converge on the theme of coming to life and that
sums up our whole faith journey as disciples of Jesus. Like the
Israelites of old, there may be times when we might be tempted
to say: 'Our hope is gone, our bones are dried up …' (Ezek 37:11)
and yet it is precisely at such a time that God breaks through to
us again through the power of the Spirit within. All this is possible through the resurrection of Jesus, for in that world-trans-
forming event the Spirit of God is made available to us all. As
Lent comes to a close, let us ask for the grace of the Holy Spirit to
understand how ours may be a dead faith needing the power of
the resurrection to make us alive to God and to our brothers and
sisters who are in need.

## (Passion Sunday) Palm Sunday

*First Reading: Isaiah 50:4-7*
These verses from the Book of the Prophet Isaiah are known as one of the Songs of the Suffering Servant. In fact this is the third song, the others being found in Is 42:1-7, Is 49:1-6 and Is 52:13-53:12. They are grouped together under this heading because they all touch on the theme of suffering which this unknown person must undergo. In its time it was thought that the person was really an embodiment of Israel, the chosen people. However, in the light of the life, death and resurrection of Jesus the early Church quickly recognised in these texts predictions of the passion and so it is particularly appropriate that one should be read today on Passion Sunday and that the last one should be in the liturgy for Good Friday. The theme of the text for today is the servant's confidence in God's presence with him even in the most adverse of circumstances. What sets him apart is the fact that he is, above all, one who listens to God's word and so is strengthened for what lies ahead.

*Second Reading: Philipians 2:6-11*
Though these beautiful verses are found in Paul's letter to the church at Philippi in northern Greece, it is generally thought that they are part of a hymn which was used in early Christian liturgy and which Paul then placed in his letter because of the relevance of the words. Just before these verses Paul is appealing to the community to be more Christ-like in their attitudes and behaviour and he then illustrates that request by highlighting the humility of Jesus, who emptied himself of the glory that was his as the Son of God and came among us as a servant, and even went so far as to undergo the agony of the cross. This loving gift of himself then issued in the glory of the resurrection in which God the Father has shown us that Jesus Christ is indeed Lord.

*Gospel: Matthew 26:14-27:66*
Holy Week, which is the high point of the Christian year, begins with two important rituals. One is the blessing of palms to recall the triumphal entry of Jesus into Jerusalem and the other is the

reading of the passion of Our Lord. They are linked because in each the identity of Jesus is acknowledged. He is the long awaited Messiah and our crucified Lord whose death on the cross shows us the lengths our loving God was prepared to go to in order to change our hearts and minds. This year we read the account of the passion according to Matthew. While the four gospels tell the story of Jesus death in a similar way, each evangelist high-lights particular scenes that are consistent with his presentation of Jesus' whole life and public ministry. So for Matthew Jesus has been presented as the fulfillment of the Jewish scriptures who is at one and the same time the Suffering Servant of Isaiah and the faithful Messiah and Son of God. At the moment of Jesus' death an earthquake occurs and the tombs of the dead are opened. These events symbolise the fact that by his death and resurrection (when another earthquake occurs) Jesus inaugur-ates the final period of human history.

*Reflection*
Suffering is part and parcel of being human and while we must readily acknowledge this fact it is also true that we usually do all in our power to avoid it. The readings for today are an invitation to reflect on how it is that passion of Jesus can change our out-look on suffering. Our Saviour is portrayed in these texts as a model of patient endurance and of faithfulness. We are not asked to believe that suffering is good in itself but we are chal-lenged to see that good can come of it and to recognise in Jesus God's solidarity with all those who endure suffering for doing what is right.

# The Season of Easter

On Easter Sunday morning we stand with the first believers at the empty tomb and wonder at what has taken place, and as we listen to the readings over the coming weeks the enormity of what we celebrate begins to dawn on us. During the Sundays of Eastertide our focus in the liturgy of the Word is entirely on the New Testament with the first reading being taken from the Acts of the Apostles instead of the Old Testament. In this way we come to see the birth of the church as being totally bound up with and inseparable from the preaching of the resurrection of Jesus. During Year A of the liturgical cycle we are also introduced to the Letter of Peter as the second reading and, as we shall see, it too is particularly appropriate for the season. The addressees of this epistle were newly baptised Christians who are being encouraged to really make their own the new faith they have embraced. Every Easter throughout the world many converts to Christianity receive the sacrament of baptism, and this serves as a reminder to us all that we too have died with Christ in order to rise with him.

## EASTER SUNDAY

*First Reading: Acts 10:37, 37-43*
Luke wrote the Acts of the Apostles as a companion volume to his gospel and it has close links to the major themes found there. Just as the gospel story brought us from Galilee to Jerusalem so the Acts will bring us from Jerusalem to Rome, thus showing the growth of the early church and the acceptance of Jesus by non-Jews. In today's reading we find Peter speaking to a group of Gentiles, the household of the centurion Cornelius, and in his speech he is offering his eyewitness account of the events surrounding the life, death and resurrection of Jesus. These verses highlight for us the central role played by the apostles and early disciples in the spread of the good news. Luke himself only came to faith in Jesus through the witness of others and so in the New Testament there is a strong emphasis on how the first disci-

ples experienced the risen Lord with them. This preaching of the resurrection is the foundation stone on which Christianity rests and Peter, the frightened man who denied even knowing Jesus, now proclaims to anyone who will listen that the risen Lord is the source of forgiveness for all who believe. It is especially significant that Peter the Jew is in a Gentile house for, in this way, he is going beyond what was permitted and is risking defilement by having such contact with non-believers. However, this is one of the fruits of the resurrection – that it breaks down the barriers between peoples.

*Second Reading: Colossians, 3:1-4*
Colossae was a city in the Roman Province of Asia and the letter addressed to the Christian community there by Paul emphasises the consequences of the resurrection of Christ for the whole world and especially for those who have been baptised. As we have already noted, the sacrament of baptism was presented as a sharing in the death of Christ so as to share in the power of his resurrection. This metaphor made sense for those who received baptism through total immersion. Going down into the water was like going into the tomb, it represented death; arising from the water was like entering a new life, the life of the risen Christ. It is this contrast that today's reading is describing. In contrasting 'earthly' and 'heavenly' realities, Paul is not asking us to us to ignore or despise our human life on earth. He is stressing that this world can only make sense viewed from a 'heavenly' perspective, in other words the perspective of the resurrection.

*Gospel: John 20:1-9*
This account of the first Easter Sunday morning is significant in that it highlights how each of us as believers must come to terms with the mystery of the resurrection. Mary reports to Peter and the beloved disciple that the tomb is empty. They in turn run to investigate and, while the disciple reaches the tomb first, he holds back in deference to Peter, the leader of the twelve. It is only when the beloved disciple enters the tomb that we are told an appropriate response to the event –'he saw and he believed'. The beloved disciple is unnamed, but in John's gospel he is present and close to Jesus at all the key moments; the Last Supper,

Calvary and now the tomb. In a sense he symbolises where all true believers should be, for each of us is called to be a beloved disciple who accompanies Jesus on his way: 'Where I am there also my servant will be' (Jn 12:26). The evangelist then makes a comment on the scene he has described by saying that 'Until now they had not understood the teaching of scripture that he must rise from the dead.' It is clear that the first disciples were not expecting the events of Easter; they were taken by surprise and then had to struggle to make sense of it. One of the key ways of doing this was to revisit the scriptures, the Old Testament, and pray about how God had been faithful to his people throughout their history. Now, through the Easter story, we have reached the highest expression of that faithfulness. 'This day was made by the Lord. We rejoice and are glad.'

*Reflection*
Our readings today bring home to us with tremendous enthusiasm and fervour how our faith life is meaningless if not rooted in the resurrection of Jesus. The gospel is not merely a story in which we are offered the good example of a man who lived a life of love. It is much more, for it shows us that God has renewed our life totally from within through the Spirit of the Risen Christ who now lives in us. This is our Easter faith so let's sing Alleluia with a full heart and voice today!

## SECOND SUNDAY OF EASTER

*First Reading: Acts 2:42-47*
This short reading is the first description of the church after the feast of the Pentecost. It follows immediately after Peter's speech on the morning of the outpouring of the Holy Spirit when he proclaims Jesus as the risen Lord for the first time. We might ask why take a reading that appears to have more to do with Pentecost than Easter? The reason is simply that in the New Testament the wonderful event of the resurrection and the gift of the Spirit are seen as inseparably linked.

The first disciples understood that, just as the Spirit of the God raised Jesus, so too will the Spirit transform all who believe in him. The evidence for that transformation is described in this reading where the early church is presented in an idealised form. The community is characterised by their fidelity to the teaching of the apostles, their sense of fellowship, the breaking of bread and prayer.

For Luke the term 'breaking of bread' relates to the Eucharist (remember the Emmaus story, Lk 24:13-35). Their unity in faith was also shown in action as they shared everything they had and no one was left in need. We are reminded that the first Christians were Jews in that, even after the resurrection of Jesus, they continued to go to the temple in Jerusalem every day. Their faith was thus nourished in private but had a very public dimension, for we are told that all the people looked up to them.

*Second Reading: 1 Peter 1:3-9*
Beginning now and lasting until the Sunday before Pentecost, we have extracts from this little known but beautifully written and inspirational letter. The opening verses state that it is addressed not just to a local church, as were several of Paul's letters, but to the Christian communities scattered throughout the Roman province of Asia (modern Turkey). From its content we may deduce that the recipients were Gentiles who had recently come to Christianity and who were experiencing some persecution because of their new-found faith. It is traditionally believed that the letter was written by Peter from Rome shortly before his martyrdom during the reign of the emperor Nero (AD64-67). The opening verses of the reading, which take the form of a prayer, are very apt for the season we are in. Peter praises God for the new life that is ours through the resurrection of Jesus. This life which begins now will come to its fullest expression in heaven and it is kept safe for us through our faith in the risen Jesus. Peter, who was an eye-witness to the events of Easter, praises and encourages the new converts because even though they have never seen Jesus they still love him and experience the joy that is at the heart of the Easter mystery.

*Gospel: John 20:19-31*
This account of an appearance of the risen Lord to the disciples follows on from his encounter with Mary Magdalen. She recognised him because he called her by name; now he is known

through the wounds of his passion: 'He showed them his hands and his side.'

These are important themes in the fourth gospel where there is a strong emphasis on faith as being rooted in a personal encounter with the Christ they have known. As if to drive that point home, we learn that Thomas is not with the others when Jesus appears to them and he steadfastly refuses to believe unless he meets the Lord for himself. When he does he too sees the wounds of the passion and he too comes to faith. However, the real aim of story becomes apparent in the words of Jesus who describes as blessed those generations of Christians whose Easter faith is not dependent on a tangible proof but on a relationship of loving trust. The evangelist then goes on to explain why he wrote his gospel: All the stories are told so that we can come to believe that Jesus does indeed reveal the love of God and, inspired by this faith, we might be fully alive as we continue on our homeward journey.

*Reflection*
These readings are a reminder to us that an Easter faith is something alive and vibrant and so they challenge us to look again at how we give expression to our belief in Christ. The philosopher Nietzsche once remarked that if Christians want others to believe in their Redeemer, why don't they look a little more redeemed? We would do well to reflect on this criticism. If we practise our religion simply as a form of insurance for the after life then we are completely failing to understand its richness and the way in which it empowers us to the full in the here and now. At Easter we are not being asked to believe in some*thing* (i.e. the resurrection), we are being asked to believe in some*one*, the crucified and risen Christ.

THIRD SUNDAY OF EASTER

*First Reading: Acts 2:14, 22-33*
We are again in chapter 2 of Acts, this time reading from Peter's powerful sermon on the feast of Pentecost. As a sign of how the apostles have been transformed by the outpouring of the Holy Spirit, Peter stands up 'with the eleven' to address the crowd.

These are the people of Jerusalem but their number is swelled by Jews from all over the country and from abroad who have made the pilgrimage for the feast in which they recalled the giving of the law to Moses on Mt Sinai. They would have known of the death of Jesus and would have considered his crucifixion a sure sign that he was not from God. It is Peter's task to persuade them otherwise. He does so by using verses from Psalm 16 which he presents to the people as a prophecy about the Messiah in which he gives thanks to God for saving him from death.

In other words, he interprets it as a prophecy about the resurrection and proclaims to the crowd that he and the other apostles are witnesses to this wonderful event. In the opening words of the sermon (not part of today's reading) he quoted from another Old Testament text to explain what was taking place. That was the prophecy from Joel in which God promises to pour out his Spirit on all flesh (Joel 3:1-5). By making these connections with the scriptures, Peter is trying to show the people that he is not offering them some fantastic story of his own making; rather he is explaining how everything was foretold and that now the scriptures are fulfilled.

*Second Reading: 1 Peter 1:17-21*
Continuing our reading from the first chapter of this letter, we now hear an appeal to the communities to live lives that are in accordance with their faith. The God they have come to know does not have favourites but judges each one on the basis of their conduct. He has won them for himself and saved them from a futile existence, not by paying a ransom in gold but through the death of Jesus.

In the ancient world kidnapping and selling people into slavery were by no means uncommon. That is the context referred to in this image of ransom. God has paid the ultimate price for them so now their lives must reflect this new reality. They can live as people of faith and hope and leave behind the fear and anxiety of the pagan world they have known for so long.

*Gospel: Luke 24:13-35*
Only in Luke do we find this resurrection story that is built around the theme of a journey. This is a theme dear to the evan-

gelist as he portrayed Jesus journeying to Jerusalem through the second half of his gospel. Now we are shown disciples coming away from Jerusalem full of disappointment and lacking in understanding. On their journey they are brought to see things differently by a Jesus they only finally recognise at the breaking of bread, and in this scene the evangelist invites us to see ourselves. He challenges us with the line 'You foolish people, slow of heart to believe,' that lies at the centre of the story and that explains what the Emmaus story is all about. Every Christian must come to a resurrection faith, one that accompanies Jesus through from Good Friday to Easter Sunday. We are invited to understand through our prayerful reading of the scriptures and the events that occur 'on the road' of our lives that the risen Lord still walks with us and meets us, especially when we gather to break bread, that is, share in the Eucharist.

*Reflection*

In the gospel of today's Mass we read of the disciples on the road to Emmaus who marvelled at how Jesus had opened up the scriptures to them: 'Did not our hearts burn within us as he explained ...?' (Lk 24:33) Jesus taught them to recognise themselves in the stories that they already knew. Unfortunately, the story of Easter may remain just a retelling of some event from the distant past if we do not allow Jesus to show us how his resurrection is a source of life for us today. Its power is to be experienced in the ordinary events of life as we struggle to be faithful. However, it is often only with hindsight that we can see the ways the Lord has accompanied us on the road. This is the work of the Spirit who lives in our hearts, so let us not be slow to ask for his help.

FOURTH SUNDAY OF EASTER

*First Reading: Acts 2:14, 36-41*

This reading follows on almost directly from last Sunday and brings us to the final part of Peter's Pentecost speech and the response of the crowd. Everything Peter said was intended to bring people to conversion and to recognise that Jesus was indeed the Christ. In this he was very successful for they turn to him wanting to know what they should do. As in the preaching of Jesus, so now in the preaching of the church the message is: 'Repent!' Behind this phrase lies the call to change one's outlook as well as the behaviour and in the wonderful atmosphere of Pentecost we are told that no less than three thousand people heeded Peter's call and were baptised. In these early chapters of the Acts there is an atmosphere of joy and enthusiasm in the description of the growth of the early church.

*Second Reading: 1 Peter 2:20-25*
It is clear from the advice given in this reading that the Christians to whom the letter was addressed were experiencing a degree of rejection and persecution on account of their faith in Jesus. Here, Peter puts before them the example of the passion of Jesus and once again relies on an Old Testament passage to explain it. This time he alludes to Isaiah 54:9 in which the suffering of the just one is the means by which the people's wounds are healed. Since Jesus endured his passion in this way, so now they must behave similarly. He did not resort to violence or abuse but put his trust in God and that is how his disciples are to live.

*Gospel: John 10:1-10*
For the next few Sundays we return to reading from John for our Eastertide gospels, though the texts are not Easter stories as such. This is a reminder to us that the person of Jesus presented to readers in these texts is always the Easter Jesus. We are not invited to believe in a man who lived a long time ago in Galilee; rather every generation of Christians is challenged to recognise that the Lord who speaks in the texts we read is present to us now. So Jesus, crucified and risen, is the door or gateway to true knowledge and love of God. The context for this unusual symbol is the wonderful story of the man born blind (chapter 9) which concludes with Jesus rebuking the Pharisees for being blind, i.e. for their lack of faith. They are the very people who see themselves as true guides and interpreters of scripture, but by their pride and presumption they are keeping people from knowing the true God whose will to save his people is unstoppable. Jesus, by contrast, is the gateway to a nourishing pasture where his disciples will find life in its fullness. We need to learn to hear his

voice among the many that call to us, to know that he is trust-worthy and to follow wherever he leads us.

*Reflection*
The excitement and joy of the first days of the church are tempered by the sober reality of the experience of persecution. These readings sum up very well the two sides of being a disciple of Jesus. The joy of Easter was only possible because of Good Friday and if we are faithful to him it is inevitable that it will cost us something. However, if our focus remains on the crucified and risen Lord then we will be able to endure whatever comes. We can learn to trust him that his deepest desire for us is that we should have life in its fullness.

## THE FIFTH SUNDAY OF EASTER

*The First Reading: Acts 6:1-7*
The situation described in this short reading illustrates to us that even in the heady days of the church after Pentecost, tensions and rivalries still emerged. Not surprisingly the differences that arose related to practical matters and had their origins in what might be called racial tensions. The Hellenists referred to here are Greek-speaking Jews from outside Palestine who were living in Jerusalem. They had their own synagogues and read from Greek versions of the scriptures. The Hebrews, on the other hand, were Jews of Palestinian origin whose spoken language was Aramaic but who used Hebrew versions of the scriptures. As we have already seen, the care for those in need was a major concern for the early Christian (Acts 2:46) and it was a failure in this area which was causing difficulties. The problem was resolved through the appointment of seven men from among the Hellenists who would take care of the needs of their own people. These became known as deacons, a term which derives from the Greek word *diakonia* meaning service. Most notable among the seven was Stephen whose ministry obviously involved more than the distribution of food for he was soon in trouble with the Jewish authorities for his preaching.

*Second Reading: 1 Peter 2:4-9*
Peter continues to exhort the Gentile converts to be true to their new calling and the best way for them to do this is to set themselves close to Christ. Using images from the Old Testament relating to building, the apostle explains how Jesus is the cornerstone of their new life and it is on this stone that they in turn are to become living stones making a spiritual dwelling for God. They are always to remember that this cornerstone of their lives was rejected by the builders yet out of that very rejection God has created for himself a new people who are a 'chosen race, a kingdom of priests, a holy people set apart to sing the praises of God'. In using this language to talk about the church, Peter is quoting the Book of Exodus where it speaks of the Israelites. In this way we see how the church saw itself as the People of God, just as the Jews had been in the Old Testament.

*Gospel: John 14:1-12*
These verses are taken from John's account of the Last Supper where Jesus speaks at length to his disciples about what it means to be his follower, both in terms of the challenge it contains and the gift that it brings. They must not be troubled by the fact that Jesus returns to the Father, (this is John's way of speaking about the passion of Jesus) because he is opening the way for each person to enter into a full relationship with God. This is expressed by the language of dwelling place, room and house. Jesus wishes us to be at home with God. This does not mean simply getting into heaven but refers rather to a whole way of life. The disciples know this way, for Jesus himself is the Way, the Truth and the Life. The use of the 'I am' phrase is an important characteristic of the fourth gospel, for by it Jesus clearly states his divine identity. It echoes the name of God found in the Old Testament where God tells Moses 'I am who I am' (Ex 3:14). Since Jesus is the truth about God, the way to God and the living embodiment of life in God, then to see and know him is to see and know God. Philip fails to grasp the point and asks to see the Father. In answer to this Jesus makes a plea for faith: 'Believe that I am in the Father and that the Father is in me.'

*Reflection*

'Set yourselves close to Christ.' No matter what the dilemma or crisis that faces the Church or indeed individual disciples within it Peter's advice cannot be improved upon. In a time of change and uncertainty many people long for old securities and the sense of stability that goes with them. Yet that is not our calling. We are to allow ourselves to be made into a community where God dwells and like the early Church in Jerusalem the universal Church today must trust that the Holy Spirit will guide it to where God wants it to be. If our hearts are troubled let us turn to Christ for in him alone is our peace.

THE SIXTH SUNDAY OF EASTER

*First Reading: Acts 8:5-8, 14-17*

This reading follows on from the story in chapter 7 of the martyrdom of Stephen and the persecution that followed it. Among those who left Jerusalem to escape the situation was Philip who brought the message of the gospel to a Samaritan town. This region is not far from Judea but in matters of faith there was great antagonism between Jews and Samaritans. This fact makes Philip's success there all the more remarkable and it is striking that his deeds are the same as those performed by Jesus. Luke, as the author of Acts, wants to show the vital connection between the life of Jesus and the life of the church. We are seeing here the first expansion of the community outside Jerusalem and this development is welcomed by Peter and John who come to see for themselves what has taken place. They pray for the gift of the Spirit as the final stage in the initiation of these new believers.

*Second Reading: 1 Peter 3:15-18*

Once again these words of Peter to the new Christians in the Roman Provinces in Asia Minor give us something of an insight into the situation which they were facing. He encourages them to always be ready to explain the reason for the hope that characterises their lives. To understand this it is important to bear in mind that in the ancient world a fatalistic view of life was widespread and the attitude of Christians, with their faith in a loving God, was in sharp contrast to the prevailing pessimistic attitude.

The early church attracted a lot of comment, much of it negative, from certain quarters, so it was essential that believers would be able to give a good account of themselves. As in the last extract we read that the key to living a good Christian life is that Christ himself should be at the heart of everything.

*Gospel: John 14:15-21*
These verses follow on directly from last Sunday's gospel and develop some of its themes. One reason why the disciples should not be troubled at Jesus' imminent departure is the promise of another advocate or paraclete. This word has its origins in legal language and refers to someone with the role of defence lawyer. The Spirit that Jesus promises will guide, teach and defend the disciples as they witness to the light among those who would choose darkness. The whole thrust of what Jesus is saying about the Spirit may be summed up by his statement: 'because I live and you will live'. The life of the risen Jesus made present through the Spirit empowers the disciples to be people of love. It is clear once again that, for the evangelist, following Jesus cannot be thought of merely in terms of keeping rules and regulations. The believer is in communion with Jesus and the Father through the work of the Spirit. These verses do not make for easy reading because of the apparently repetitive style but they provide rich fare indeed for quiet prayer in preparation for Pentecost as we invite the Holy Spirit to enlighten our minds with true understanding.

*Reflection*
In a certain sense we have a lot in common with the early church even though we are separated from it by a span of nearly two thousand years. We live now in a post-Christian society and believers are being asked to account for their faith in an increasingly secular and sometimes hostile environment. This is not necessarily a bad thing if it forces us to think deeply about what we really believe and what difference it makes to our lives and the lives of others. In such circumstances it is important that we really understand our faith so that we can be credible witnesses in a world which is deeply in need of the compassionate love and enduring hope that only Jesus can bring.

THE ASCENSION OF THE LORD

*First Reading: Acts 1:1-11*
The opening verses of the Acts of the Apostles offer us not only a description of the ascension but also an insight into how the evangelist Luke saw the relationship between the time of Jesus and the time of the church. The life of Jesus culminated in his death and resurrection in Jerusalem and now from there the church will bring this good news to the world. Only Luke tells us of the period of forty days after the resurrection during which Jesus continued to speak to the apostles and to prepare them for the gift of the Spirit. From their question to him it is clear that they expect the end of the world to be soon, but Jesus emphasises that they are not to worry themselves about such issues, rather they are to concentrate on being his witnesses throughout the world. This will be possible because they will be clothed with power from on high and just as the ministry of Jesus was driven and guided by the Holy Spirit, so too will theirs.

*Second Reading: Ephesians 1:17-23*
This reading does not specifically talk about the ascension of Jesus but it is offered to us today so that we might reflect on what the feast means. The focus of today's celebration is not so much on Jesus' departure as on his return to the Father. At the right hand of God Jesus now rules over all creation by the power of God that raised him from the dead, and there is no force in the universe that can ever come between him and those who believe. The 'Sovereignty, Power, Authority and Domination' of which Paul speaks are forces which Jews believed to be at work in creation, more powerful than the merely human but always under the control of God. Paul prays for the faithful that they may come to understand the incredible thing that God has done in raising Jesus from the dead and how they are all drawn into the very life of God through being part of the body of Christ which is the church.

*Gospel: Matthew 28:16-20*
It is worth noting that Luke's is the only gospel to give us the story of the Ascension of Our Lord and for him it is important

because it prepares the way for Pentecost and the presence of Jesus in the church through the gift of the Holy Spirit. Matthew deals with this reality in a different way. At the beginning of his gospel the child to be born is called 'Emmanuel, a name which means God is with us'. As the story of Jesus' life unfolded, the ways in which God is with us became increasingly clear through the activity of Jesus preaching the kingdom, healing, and bringing forgiveness. Now having been through the experience of his death and resurrection, Jesus announces their mission to his apostles and encourages them in it by telling them that he is with them always, to the end of time. The life of the church only makes sense if it is rooted in and driven forward by an awareness of that presence.

*Reflection*
We are reminded today that it is not the task of Christians to 'stand looking up into the sky' either to mourn Jesus' departure from earth or to simply await his return. Our role until his Second Coming is to witness to his presence still in the world through the community of faith that believes in him. This we do through recognising that we have indeed been clothed with power from on high. As his body the church we are to be Jesus' continued presence on earth bringing freedom, healing and forgiveness to all who long to know the true God.

PENTECOST SUNDAY

*First Reading: Acts 2:1-11*
At the time of Jesus the Jews celebrated the feast of Pentecost on the fiftieth day after Passover. In it they recalled the gift of the Law to Moses on Mount Sinai. This Law embodied the covenant, which made them the people of God, and so the feast was a joyful celebration of their identity. It was one of the pilgrimage feasts in Judaism that required people to make the effort to come to the temple in Jerusalem. It is in the context of this feast that Luke presents the birth of the new people of God with the outpouring of the Holy Spirit on the apostles. The original feast now takes on a whole new meaning as the Spirit of God appears as tongues of fire resting on each of the apostles. According to an

old Jewish tradition, God spoke with fire on Mt Sinai to all the peoples of the world but only Israel accepted. Now, however, through the gift of the Spirit God speaks again to people from all over the world and this time they hear and understand. The sin of Babel, which divided the nations, is now undone as those who have gathered in Jerusalem for the feast are full of wonder at what is taking place.

*Second Reading: 1 Cor 12:3-7, 12-13*
As we saw earlier in the year when reading from First Corinthians, the church in Corinth was suffering from petty rivalries and faction fighting. Paul, in attempting to deal with the problem, now reminds them why there is neither need for jealousy nor room for pride since everything they have is a gift of God through the Spirit in baptism. Each person has a God-given talent that is for the good of the community and in this way they are all dependent on each other to make up the one body that is Christ. So the Spirit is both the source of unity and diversity within the church.

*Gospel: John 20:19-23*
Since Matthew does not speak of the giving of the Spirit in his gospel, we turn to John for the reading today. The fourth evangelist rolls the events of Holy Week and Pentecost into one ongoing act of loving re-creation on the part of God. We are invited to see in Jesus, exalted on the cross, the total self-giving of God and we are also asked to receive from Jesus risen his Easter gift of *Shalom*, peace. This is bestowed on us when Jesus, the Eternal Word, breathes on us and makes a new creation, just as God breathed a breath of life into the first man in Genesis 2:7. At the heart of the transformation wrought by the Spirit is the gift of forgiveness which is for everyone, even though some may choose to reject it. This is the meaning of the phrase: 'Whose sins you shall retain they are retained.'

*Reflection*
The gift of the Spirit is the great leveller as we all equally become the children of God. Birthdays are happy occasions or at least they should be! Today as we look back at almost two thousand

years of the church we can see much evidence of the work of the Spirit in the lives of countless Christians who have opened themselves up to the power of the Spirit within them. Unfortunately we can also see evidence of the refusal to humbly acknowledge how we have been blessed. The problems, which dogged the community in Corinth, have not gone away. Today, however, we can celebrate this birthday with Paul's words calling us again to recognise that we are indeed the body of Christ and that our calling is to do good for one another. The challenge is to live an ongoing Pentecost as human beings made anew in the image and likeness of God.

# Feasts of the Lord in Ordinary Time

*The Feasts of Trinity Sunday and The Body and Blood of the Lord are celebrated in Ordinary Time on the two Sundays following Pentecost.*

## TRINITY SUNDAY

*First Reading: Exodus 34:4-6, 8-9*
It is a sad fact that for many Christians the God revealed in the covenant at Sinai is at best merely just and at worst downright vengeful, but such a belief does not respect what is in the text. So today we have these striking verses from the Book of Exodus in which God reveals himself to Moses. To understand their full significance it is worth going back a little to 33:18 where Moses asks to see the glory of God. His prayer is answered as God passes him by on the mountain and proclaims himself as Yahweh, the God of tenderness and compassion. Yet the context for this revelation is mysterious. God may not be seen by Moses face to face but he allows him to glimpse his back as he passes by. Along with this revelation is the promise to go with the chosen people on their journey. It is as though the Bible says that Moses can only see Yahweh's back because he is following where he leads. Coming to know God is a journey of faith.

*Second Reading: 2 Corinthians 13:11-13*
In this short reading we have the concluding verses of Paul's second letter to the church in Corinth. They are particularly appropriate today because they show the connection between how we live and what we believe. As always, Paul is ending his letter with an appeal for authentic gospel living in the community. Such a life would be characterised by peace and love and it is made possible through the work of the blessed Trinity in their midst: the grace of Christ which brings them the love of God which in turn is made known to them through the sharing of the Holy Spirit.

*Gospel: John 3:16-18*
There is no mention of the Trinity as such in the scriptures. However, the Christian doctrine of the Trinity that affirms there

are three persons in the one God is totally rooted in the teaching of the New Testament. As the church reflected on the mystery of God revealed in the life, death and resurrection of Jesus, the awareness grew that God is a communion of love and that we are invited into that communion to find our true worth as human beings. The gospel for today highlights the positive aspect this teaching by asserting that God sent his Son out of love but it also acknowledges the tension created by the fact that we are free to reject this love. We may decide we are self-sufficient and if we do we are lost – not because God wants us to be, but because we are trying to be something we are not.

*Reflection*
The novelist Graham Greene once said that he would not be able to believe in a God he could understand. Today we are brought before the mystery of the God who is a Trinity of love and, like Moses, the only appropriate response is to bow down and worship and to continue to follow in faith, confident that we are journeying towards the fullness of life. Today's feast is not intended to baffle us with the unknowable. Nor do we have to get our heads around this mystery, we need only leave our hearts open to what is revealed, namely that our God is a communion of love in whom we are invited to share.

## THE BODY AND BLOOD OF CHRIST

*First Reading: Deuteronomy 8:2-3, 14-16*
The name Deuteronomy means 'second law' and the book is called this because it visits again the giving of the Law to the Israelites, a story that has already been told in Exodus. This time it is framed within a last will and testament of Moses who, before they enter the Promised Land, reminds the people of all they have been through. The verses in today's reading sum this up very well and are also very appropriate for the feast we are celebrating. Moses recalls the fact that though they were hungry and thirsty in the wilderness, God never abandoned them but taught them that they must learn to have faith in the continuing presence of their saving Lord with them. In Deuteronomy the readers are frequently asked to 'remember' – it is a key word for

them in establishing their identity as the People of God. When they remember the Exodus during Passover they make present again the saving action of God. This point is of great significance for Christian understanding of the Eucharist and the saving action of Jesus which it makes present.

*Second Reading: 1 Corinthians 10:16-17*
The context for these for these vital words of Paul is the strained and difficult relationships that exist in the community in Corinth. Some people there are still participating in pagan rituals and eating food that has been sacrificed to idols. They argue that since the idols are meaningless there is no religious significance to be attached to eating the food. Paul replies that their focus should be on what they do at the Eucharist. By participating in the bread and the cup they are uniting themselves to Christ and to the whole Christian community, therefore any action that harms or threatens the unity of the church is to be avoided. There can be no such thing as a private sharing in the body and blood of the Lord. The Eucharist is the sacrament of our unity as the Body of Christ.

*Gospel: John 6:51-58*
The Fourth Gospel gives no account of the Eucharist at the last supper. Instead in chapter 6 the evangelist uses the occasion of the multiplication of the loaves and fishes to reflect on the ident-ity of Jesus as the Bread of Life. In the biblical tradition bread is a very important symbol going back to the manna in the wilder-ness and later in the books of Proverbs and Sirach where it is a symbol for the wisdom of God. In these writings it is offered as nourishment to those who would seek to know God and to do his will. It is against this background that we read today's gospel in which Jesus affirms that he is the wisdom of God, the bread of life, the one who, by means of his life, death and resurrection, nourishes our deepest hunger for God. The way we come to him is by faith and that is supremely expressed in the act of sharing in the Eucharist. In this way, we draw life from Jesus even as he drew life from the Father.

*Reflection*

Today's feast is an opportunity for the church to reflect on the wonderful mystery of the Eucharist, the sacrament that nourishes our faith and unites us as the People of God. Each of the readings offers us opportunities to pray about its significance and they are reminders of the richness of this tradition in the church. They all remind us that this mystery cannot be separated from the way we live our lives. If we wish to show reverence for Christ in the Eucharist then we must show reverence for Christ in our community. To separate them is to risk idolatry!

# Ordinary Time

*First Reading: Is 42:1-4, 6-7*

In the middle section of the Book of Isaiah there are four passages which are known as the Servant's Songs. It is thought that they originally referred to those few Israelites who were a faithful remnant to the covenant at the time of the exile in Babylon. This is the first of these songs and in it Israel is referred to as 'my servant' and 'the one in whom my soul delights'. It is not hard to see how these texts were later taken up by the church as referring to Jesus. It is the work of God's anointed (the messiah) to bring justice, and to do this he must be filled with the Spirit of God. Such a figure won't succeed by force of arms, rather he will achieve his aim by being faithful to God. Through his gentleness the eyes of the blind will be opened and the captives will be freed. These verses combine to give a moving summary of what Jesus' ministry will be and so it is appropriate that they be read on the feast of the baptism when Jesus begins his public ministry with an outpouring of the Holy Spirit and when God the Father acknowledges him as 'the one in whom my soul delights'.

*Second Reading: Acts 10:34-38*

This very important passage from the Acts of the Apostles marks a significant shift for the early church. Under the inspiration of the Holy Spirit, Peter goes to the house of Cornelius, a Roman centurion and a Gentile, and there baptises him and his family. They are the first non-Jews to receive the Spirit in baptism and even for Peter this is a day of momentous importance for only now does he begin to understand that the message of Jesus Christ, who is the Lord of all people, is to be preached to the whole world. In explaining who Jesus is to his Gentile audience, Peter begins by talking about the baptism in the Jordan for this marked the occasion when Jesus, 'anointed with the Holy Spirit and with power', began to bring the good news to all who would receive it.

*Gospel: Matthew 3:13-17*

The scene of the Baptism of Jesus is prepared for in Matthew by the description of John the Baptist that precedes it. He is like the prophets of old and even his clothing of camel's hair is like that of Elijah. When the people come to John for baptism they are seeking a ritual cleansing and showing their desire to repent. However, John preaches about the one who will baptise them with the Holy Spirit. Hence it is somewhat surprising when Jesus seeks baptism from John. By doing so, Jesus is taking his place with sinful humanity and this is the meaning of his strange words to John, that 'all righteousness should be fulfilled'. Righteousness in the Bible frequently refers to correct moral behaviour, but it can also refer to God's saving activity on our behalf. In Jesus 'God is with us' as we were told in the infancy story. Now, at the moment of baptism, we see how Jesus identifies fully with our broken race and yet is filled with the Holy Spirit. Through him we will be saved by one like ourselves, moved by the Spirit to know and do God's will.

*Reflection*

In the liturgy for today, which begins the season of Ordinary Time, we are invited to recall our own baptism and to recognise in it the drama of God's extraordinary power at work in our lives. At our baptism each one of us became the beloved of God in whom his soul delights and so each of us must try to live as people filled with the Spirit, that Spirit whose work is so beautifully described in these readings.

THE SECOND SUNDAY IN ORDINARY TIME

*First Reading: Isaiah 49:3, 5-6*

The first reading is another of the Servant Songs from Isaiah and this time the theme follows on from what we read last week. The servant of God is once again portrayed as someone specially honoured by God and who in turn places all his trust in God. From the very outset he has been set aside as God's servant with a task to perform and this was usually seen as bringing the Israelites back to their God (note how the name Jacob is often used to refer to the whole people of Israel). However, that mission is now widened to include all peoples so that Israel will become a light to the nations guiding everyone to a knowledge of the Lord. The early church saw in the ministry of Jesus a fulfillment of this prophecy. Jesus is the true servant of God and through his life, death and resurrection the whole world will come to share in the salvation promised to Israel.

*Second Reading: 1 Corinthians 1:1-3*
This Sunday we begin reading from the first letter of Paul to the Christian community in Corinth. We know from the Acts of the Apostles that Paul founded the community in Corinth and that he spent about 18 months there probably between AD 50 and 52 (Acts 18:1-19:1). Later, while he was staying at Ephesus (between AD 54 and 56) he had occasion to write to the Corinthians on a number of occasions though only two of the letters have survived. In this first one it is clear that he is trying to deal with factions and rivalries which have emerged in the community. The letter begins in the style which is typical of the period, whereby Paul introduces himself and those with him. In this case it is Sosthenes, about whom nothing is known. He reminds them that he was appointed by God to be an apostle and that they in turn are called to take their place among the saints (i.e. all the baptised). These are important details because some in Corinth are disputing Paul's leadership and also their factions are leading to a break-up of the church as we shall see very soon.

*Gospel: John 1:29-34*
The theme of the Baptism of Jesus is returned to here, though this time it is from the gospel of John. While Matthew, Mark and Luke follow a similar style in reporting what Jesus did, John uses a different style to explore the question of who Jesus is. In this short text we have the reflections of John the Baptist on Jesus' identity. He calls Jesus 'the Lamb of God who takes away the sins of the world'. In doing so he recalls the Passover lamb of the Exodus and also the person foretold in Isaiah as the Suffering Servant, who was like a lamb led to the slaughter. Through the symbolic language that is so typical of the Fourth Gospel, John testifies to knowing Jesus not only as the Lamb of God but also as the Son of God. On other words he knows him not only in terms of what he came to do but also for who he is.

*Reflection*
We too need to know Jesus not just for what he did but also as a person who lives now. As disciples we do not just observe rules, we are friends (Jn 15:15) because Jesus wants us to know him and the Father who sent him. Our baptism initiated us into this relationship but it is up to us to nourish it through prayer, the Eucharist and our loving service of one another. As with John the Baptist, if we know Jesus then our lives will testify to it. The squabbles which emerged among the believers in Corinth were a scandal and a betrayal of the good news. So as we reflect on these readings, let us thank God for the parish or local community to which we belong and let us ask God's blessing on all who are working there to build up the Body of Christ which is his church.

THE THIRD SUNDAY IN ORDINARY TIME

*First Reading: Isaiah 8:23-9:3*
This reading, or at least a part of it, was used during midnight Mass at Christmas and then the emphasis was on the role of the messiah as the one who would inaugurate a time of peace and plenty. Today we return to the text but this time we include the verse found at the beginning. This refers to the tribes of Zebulun and Naphtali and their territories, which were in the region which corresponds to Galilee. At the time of the prophet Isaiah this area was devastated by the invasion of the Assyrians. The prophet looks forward to a time when it will be transformed, and the evangelist Matthew points out to us that when Jesus began his ministry in Galilee that time had come. It was import-ant to make this connection because few people in first-century Palestine would have imagined the territory of Galilee as a focus for the activity of the messiah. It was much more under Gentile influence than Jerusalem and Judea, where it seemed much more likely that the messiah would appear. Matthew wants to emphas-ise that Jesus is the fulfillment of the scriptures and so in the gospel for today, which marks the beginning of Jesus' public life in Galilee, the evangelist shows that with Jesus 'a light has dawned' for the people who lived in darkness.

*Second Reading: 1 Corinthians 1:10-13, 17*
Paul wastes no time in getting to the heart of the matter in his letter to the church in Corinth. He has heard from a source in the community that there are serious differences among them. The source is named as Chloe's people but we know nothing about them. However, they have informed Paul about the factions that have arisen whereby groups are claiming different personalities as their leader. The Cephas referred to is Peter (Cephas being the Aramaic version of his name), while Apollos is known from Acts 18:23-19:1. Paul is clearly annoyed with them for such divisions and takes no pleasure from his own name being used. He argues that he is for Christ and that all of them have been baptised only in Christ's name. He then prepares for the next phase of his reply to them by saying that his own role was as a preacher, and not a preacher of some philosophy or other but of the message of the cross.

*Gospel: Matthew 4:12-23*
In this text we read of the beginning of Jesus' public ministry in Galilee. As with all the significant moments in Jesus' ministry in Matthew, the evangelist is at pains to point out that the scriptures are fulfilled by him. This is important, because there would have been no general expectation that the Messiah would come from Galilee and Matthew wants his Jewish-Christian readers to be in no doubt that Jesus is indeed they one for whom they have waited. Fittingly, Jesus' preaching begins where John left off and is an echo of what John had said: 'Repent for the kingdom of heaven is close at hand.' The theme of the kingdom is a favourite one of Matthew and its meaning must be understood properly if we are to appreciate all the richness of Matthew's account of Jesus' life. The other evangelists call it the kingdom of God, but Matthew's preference for the term heaven is an indicator of his Jewish background. In Jewish tradition the use of God's name is avoided wherever possible, out of respect, and hence Matthew's use of the word heaven. The phrase refers to God's reign or rule on earth and not to paradise or the end time. It is not, however, a political or geographical entity, rather it comes about when God's will is done and that is what Jesus' life and preaching is all about. It is striking that Jesus' first action

after proclaiming the kingdom is to call disciples because the task of witnessing to the kingdom is not something done by Jesus alone – rather he calls disciples who will share in and continue this work. The call is presented in radical terms – leaving everything to follow him. This is because the kingdom of heaven is a radical option, often at odds with the way of the world and its values.

*Reflection*

The readings point to two very different realities which are a part of the experience of hearing the good news. The gospel, when properly heard and understood, is a source of unspeakable joy – it is a message of liberation which frees us from the darkness both within and without. Yet all too easily we are tempted, as were the Christians in Corinth, to use it as something which makes us somehow better than others or superior to them in some way. We quickly forget that at the heart of the message is the cross, a symbol of humiliation and degradation. Today let us acknowledge with Paul that 'We are for Christ', and let us pray that this will always be the focus of our faith as we seek to bring about the kingdom that Jesus has announced and inaugurated

## THE FOURTH SUNDAY IN ORDINARY TIME

*First Reading: Zephaniah 2:3, 3:12-13*

The prophet Zephaniah preached just before the time of Jeremiah (ca 640BC). The country had been under foreign domination and many had abandoned their faith in the Lord. The book of Zephaniah is a warning that the 'day of the Lord' will come. This is a time when God will re-establish his rule and when the humble who seek to do God's commands will live under his protection. The long-awaited day of the Lord and the coming of his kingdom are shown to occur in the words and deeds of Jesus. Today's gospel of the beatitudes is a restatement of the values mentioned by the prophet Zephaniah. The major difference between them is how this kingdom comes about. The prophet imagined a day of God's anger; Jesus, however, shows us that it will be love that conquers.

*Second Reading: 1 Corinthians 1:26-31*
Paul, in an effort to bring the proud and arrogant Christians of Corinth to their senses, reminds the community that it is not made up of people who have anything to boast about. God did not choose them because they were the leading lights of the city, rather it was the opposite. They were chosen because they had more reason than most to appreciate the power of the good news. Within their own society they were on the margins, yet it was to them that Christ has been made known. They have become members of his body and in him they have found wisdom, holiness and true freedom. So instead of boasting about which leader they are following, let them simply proclaim what God has done for them.

*Gospel: Matthew 5:1-12*
This passage marks the beginning of the Sermon on the Mount, a key section of Matthew's gospel in which the moral teaching of the kingdom of God is presented. It takes up some three chapters and opens with today's text in which the values of the kingdom are summarised in the beatitudes. That this sermon is given on a mountain may suggest that, just as Moses gave the Law on Mount Sinai, so now Jesus proclaims the new law. In the first three beatitudes, groups normally considered in need of pity are in fact esteemed. The poor in spirit, the meek and those who mourn are those who reject the way of the world with its arrogance, oppression and superficial pleasures. Jesus declares that the kingdom and its joy will be experienced by those who put their trust in God. Those who mourn are not those who are gloomy but rather those who realise that the world is not as it is meant to be. Our true happiness lies in yearning for righteousness, in showing mercy, working for peace and in having an undivided heart. Choosing the way of the kingdom will lead to difficulties and persecution but this need not deter us; rather it should be a source of joy for it means that we share in the great tradition of the prophets.

*Reflection*
In these readings we can see that people need to be reminded of the essentials. The Israelites had wandered away from God and

would only find their way to him by rediscovering the importance of living honest and just lives. The early Christians are very quickly forgetting that their new-found faith rests not on anything they have done but entirely on the wonderful generosity of God. So the appropriate response to the gift of faith is a humble gratitude and an earnest desire to simply live it out. That type of lifestyle is summed up perfectly in the beatitudes and is perfectly lived out in all that Jesus said and did.

### THE FIFTH SUNDAY IN ORDINARY TIME

*First Reading: Isaiah 58:7-10*
The Book of the Prophet Isaiah is the longest in the Bible and the writings from chapter 40 onwards refer to times long after the death of the prophet himself (ca 695BC). This happened because subsequent generations so valued his thought that they did not hesitate to include later material which was in keeping with the teaching of their great master. The verses we read today illustrate as well as any in the Bible one of the most valuable insights of the prophets of Israel, and that is that there can be no true religion without justice and a genuine concern for the poor. The instructions which are given reflect the commands of the covenant but they also stress that if we want to know God and be close to him, then we must first seek to care for those around us. By doing this, the wounds inflicted by our own selfishness are healed and we will become a source of light and hope for those around us. This imagery is picked up in today's gospel when Jesus calls his disciples the light of the world.

*Second Reading: 1 Corinthians 2:1-5*
In chapter 1 of the letter, we saw how Paul needed to remind the community in Corinth that the divisions among them were inconsistent with their faith in Christ. He reminded them of their humble origins and that they had nothing to boast about when it came to saying whose side they were on. Now, still looking back to their beginnings, he asks them to remember how it was that he himself arrived among them. We can get an insight into what he is talking about if we bear in mind that Paul came to Corinth from Athens where he had failed miserably to win over the

intellectual elite of that great city when he preached in the Aeropagus (see Acts 17). It was a humbled and chastened Paul who introduced the Corinthians to the message of the gospel. This he did neither by eloquent oratory, nor with highbrow philosophy but rather by proclaiming the crucified Christ and relying on the power of the Spirit. Recalling those days should now serve to help the Corinthians see the shamefulness of their current disputes and to realise that what matters is that they have a shared faith, not in Paul or Apollos or any other local leader, but in Christ himself who died on the cross to make them one.

*Gospel: Matthew 5:13-16*
In this short reading, Jesus relies on two images, salt and light, to drive home the significance of being a disciple. In telling them they are the salt of the earth, Jesus is speaking in a context where the vital role of salt is readily understood. It was used as a spice and a preservative and was present in every household. If, however, it became insipid it had to be thrown out. This is a forceful image for the community; it is a reminder that their calling is not for themselves, they are disciples for the sake of the world. Should they ignore this truth then they no longer serve any purpose. The second image, that of light, is a universal one and has already been employed in the gospel. In the infancy story, the wise men followed a bright star and in 4:16 Jesus was likened to a light shining on people who had sat in darkness. Now that image is transferred to his disciples. By means of their lives they will bring people to an awareness of God's goodness and the value of the kingdom proclaimed by Jesus.

*Reflection*
These readings have an immediate relevance for our Christian faith today and for communities everywhere. All too easily we can become absorbed in ourselves and our own little circle and can end up by taking pride in what we see as our successes and feeling superior to others. Meanwhile Christ in the poor is ignored as we concentrate on our lovely liturgies. We can quickly forget that our calling is to become Christ, to die to ourselves and to live for others. It is only in this way that our Sunday Eucharist makes sense. We are challenged here to recognise

where the Lord has let his light shine in our lives and in a spirit of gratitude allow that light to reach others through us.

THE SIXTH SUNDAY IN ORDINARY TIME

*First Reading: Ecclesiasticus 15:15-20*
We have already had a reading from the Book of Ecclesiasticus (also known as Sirach, its title in Hebrew) this year and that was just after Christmas, on the Feast of the Holy Family. As we noted then it is one of the latest books of the Old Testament, written around the year 200BC. The author was aware of the growing influence of Greek culture and philosophy in the Palestine of his time and so he set about writing a defence of the biblical worldview in which he stressed the importance of recognising that in the Law of Moses Israel had been gifted with the very wisdom of God. In the verses we read today, there is an emphasis on the freedom of the individual to choose between right and wrong. What is at issue here is life and death and each person must decide what it is they want. Life is to be found in doing God's will, death is the consequence of sin. In saying this the author is echoing teaching found elsewhere in the Old Testament (see Deut 30:19). However, he goes a step further when he insists that God has given no-one permission to sin. While such a statement may seem self evident to us, we should bear in mind that in earlier parts of the Old Testament it appears that God is in some way responsible for sin (see Ex 11:10, 2 Sam 24:1). With this assertion the author is ruling out any notion of predestination. Each one of us is to be held accountable for his or her actions.

*Second Reading: 1 Corinthians 2:6-10*
These verses follow on directly from last Sunday and show Paul developing the theme of wisdom or philosophy which he had touched upon then. At the heart of the good news is a wisdom which is not accessible to the powerful nor to those who might be considered wise in the eyes of the world. For what Paul is teaching is the wisdom of God which has been revealed through the Spirit. What then is this? In an effort to portray its wonder and power Paul, in a rather free way, combines two Old

Testament texts which suggest that what God has planned for those who love him is way beyond our wildest dreams. However, by the work of the Spirit this is precisely what has been revealed and it is the gospel of Jesus. It is the Holy Spirit who makes it possible for the community to understand the true meaning of the cross and resurrection and, if they were open to the action of the Spirit, they would be acting in a more mature way and responding to the gift which they have been given instead of squabbling among themselves.

*Gospel: Matthew 5:17-37*
In this long extract from the Sermon on the Mount, Jesus is speaking to people who are well aware of the commandments of the Law. However, he insists that in their attitudes and behaviour they must go beyond a mere legal observance. In speaking here about righteousness he is talking about acting according to the will of God and so, when it comes to anger, adultery, divorce and oaths, Jesus is stressing the radical demands of the kingdom. It is pointless condemning murder and adultery when the attitudes that lead to murder and adultery, such as anger and lust, are left unchecked in our own lives. In his time divorce was easily obtained by men and Jesus condemns this approach which involves a devaluing of married love (it is a theme returned to in Mt 19:1-15). So too he tackles the way oaths employing the name of God are used to show one's sincerity, but for many this practice has become a source of hypocrisy. In all the examples given, Jesus is not writing a new law – rather he is challenging us to get beyond a morality which is happy to ask the question: how far can I go or what can I get away with? He wants us to look humbly into our hearts and to admit our need of help in living as God wants us to.

*Reflection*
In an age when the notion of sin is downplayed and our willingness to accept personal responsibility for our actions appears to be on the wane, the straight talking from the Book of Ecclesiasticus may come as something of a shock. Yet when we think about it, can we deny its truth? If we live our lives blaming God, our circumstances or others for our behaviour then we are

opting out and the very challenging message of Jesus in the Sermon on the Mount will make no sense to us. However, the truth that we have free will must also stand with the gift of God's grace which we receive through the Holy Spirit. Left to ourselves we often fail to do what we know is right and that is why we must sincerely turn to God and seek his help in living the morality of the kingdom which is both a gift and a challenge to all believers.

## THE SEVENTH SUNDAY IN ORDINARY TIME

*First Reading: Leviticus 19:1-2, 17-19*
The Book of Leviticus is the third book of the Bible and is made up of laws and commandments relevant to worship and every-day living. It is sometimes mistakenly believed by Christians that it was Jesus who introduced the command of love of neigh-bour but, as today's reading shows, this teaching was firmly rooted in the tradition of the Jews. A point to note in this short text is the emphasis on the reason given for not bearing hatred, nor holding grudges. The Lord their God has shown himself to them through freeing them from oppression in Egypt. In this way he manifested his holiness and they, as his people, must as-pire to be like him. So when God commands them to love their neighbour and follows it with 'I am the Lord', it is not as though he is merely saying 'you have to do this because I am in charge' – rather he is saying your very existence and identity depends on you striving to follow in my way of covenant love and justice.

*Second Reading: 1 Corinthians 3:16-23*
Paul continues in his efforts to make the Christians in Corinth see that their divisions, based on arrogance and self importance, are contrary to the core values of the gospel. He reminds them that as a community they are the temple of God and by using this image he is suggesting that by their factions and infighting they are destroying something holy. He then returns to the theme of wisdom which is clearly part of the problem in Corinth. Some people imagine themselves to be superior to others by virtue of their 'wisdom' but Paul reminds them that the gospel message is foolishness by the standards of the world

and so they too must learn to embrace this foolishness. Christ emptied himself to become their servant and they, as his followers, are to follow the example of humility that made Christ into their servant so that they can learn to be servants too.

*Gospel: Matthew 5:38-48*
While the Old Testament teaching of an eye for an eye is considered to be primitive, in its time it represented progress because it restricted the punishment to fitting the crime. However, in the next part of the Sermon on the Mount Jesus shows that the morality of the kingdom of God demands of us that we abandon all thought of revenge. Once again Jesus places the focus on the attitude and behaviour of the disciple, stressing that forgetfulness of self is what is demanded. He then refers to the Old Testament teaching in today's first reading and goes to show the way it had become distorted. The Bible nowhere says you must hate your enemy but this attitude is present is places and this is what Jesus confronts head on by saying that his followers must love their enemies and pray for those who persecute them. And the reason for such an extreme demand? So that they may become truly children of their Father. God grants nature's blessings on both the bad and the good and it is this perfection of love to which the disciples must aspire. Loving those who love you is no great achievement, even those outside the community of Israel can do that (hence the reference to tax collectors and Gentiles). By contrast, those who would enter the kingdom must be motivated by the highest ideal: the perfect love of God.

*Reflection*
The readings today may well stop us in our tracks because they present the highest calling of the Christian and in terms that may seem well nigh impossible. However, we should remember that the gospel is 'good news' and Jesus is not looking for more ways to make us feel guilty. Sermon on the Mount is not just about us, it is also about the nature of God and the kingdom he wills for us. Jesus' whole mission derives from his understanding of his Father's universal and infinite love. He is not asking the impossible; he is setting us an example in his own life and also empowering us to walk that same path. He is challenging

us to open ourselves up the love that can make us truly loving people. Today's Eucharist invites us to pray for this gift.

## THE EIGHTH SUNDAY IN ORDINARY TIME

*First Reading: Isaiah 49:14-15*
The context for this short extract is the Jewish people's experience of defeat in war and exile in Babylonia in the sixth century BC. With their temple destroyed and their enemies victorious, it would be reasonable to think that perhaps their God had abandoned them. In the opening verse we are told it is Zion who is saying this. This is the name of the hill on which Jerusalem was built and it became another name for the Holy City. However, in the midst of their sadness and despair the prophet speaks a word of profound consolation using that most universal of images: a mother's love for her baby. God's love for his people is yet more faithful than this. The prophet is urging them to see beyond present difficulties, however extreme, and to trust that God will act on their behalf and bring good out of evil.

*Second Reading: 1 Corinthians 4:1-5*
Paul has written a long appeal to the Corinthians to try and explain to them why what is taking place among them is inconsistent with their Christian identity. He has reminded them that Christ must be their model and focus and in this way they can begin to overcome their divisions. Now in this part of the letter he is preparing to deal with some of the specific moral problems that have been brought to his attention. Before he gives his opinion he spends a little time explaining why he should be listened to at all. He is at pains to point out that he works as a 'steward of the mysteries', a steward being someone given the task of overseeing the running of the house. He affirms that he is worthy of their trust in the task that he has undertaken and is happy to let God be his judge. The reason Paul needs to say these things is that there are some in the community who are not particularly happy with him. His difficulties with them will become more apparent in his second letter to them, which is very focused on this theme of stewardship.

*Gospel: Matthew 6:24-34*
The readings from the Sermon on the Mount continue this week with the emphasis moving towards the need to trust in God. The opening verse about money provides the context for all that is said: if we are concerned about amassing wealth then our priorities are mistaken. We cannot take seriously the values of the kingdom if we do not put our trust in God. The word 'mammon' is Aramaic and means wealth or property. In his appeal to trust in providence Jesus asks a series of short, direct questions that help to put the whole issue in focus. 'Is not life more than food and the body more than clothing?' 'Are you not more important than the birds of the air?' 'Can any of you add a moment to your span of life by worrying?' The questions are simple and the answers obvious but if we don't reflect on these themes we will continue to be driven by worries that prevent us from enjoying the present moment and living gratefully in it.

*Reflection*
We live in a world where advertising agencies and the companies that employ them spend billions using every technique imaginable to persuade us that our well being, happiness and health all depend on having the product they are trying to sell. The world was simpler in Jesus time but the basic human need for security and certainty was no less a part of people's mindset. So the words of the gospel today, rooted as they are in the imagery found in Isaiah, are an invitation to us to think deeply about the basics and what is driving us. Jesus is not suggesting that we just ignore our human needs but he is telling us we need to prioritise them. The way to do this is to think first about God's will for the world (the kingdom) and to let that be our concern. There we will find a capacity to trust in God and the energy to live life to the full.

THE NINTH SUNDAY IN ORDINARY TIME

*First Reading: Deuteronomy 11:18, 26-32, 32*
The Book of Deuteronomy is the last book of the Pentateuch and concludes the Torah or Law. As such, it is a vital summary of what is required of the Israelites to fulfil their mission and iden-

tity as the People of God. In this reading we find an appeal to the people that the words of the covenant that God has made with them should be ever present to them, and this commandment is literally obeyed by orthodox Jews to this day. At prayer time they wear small boxes attached to their head and hands as a symbol of their desire to live by the Law of Moses. Behind the exhortation to put the Law first is an awareness of free will and that we all have the power to choose. God asks his people to choose life, to live by what he has made known to them and to reject the selfish and oppressive ways of the world that he has saved them from. The curse referred to is not then something actively perpetrated by a jealous God who wants to bully people into submission, but a simple recognition that living by the ways of selfishness and oppression brings misery.

*Second Reading: Romans 3:21-25, 25*
In the letter to the Romans, Paul is trying to persuade both Gentiles and Jews in that community of their total dependence on Christ for the salvation they desire. The context for this debate is the fact that the Jews would have looked down on the Gentiles as pagan and incapable of being saved, while the Gentiles may have considered themselves as superior, not bound by rules and regulations. For both parties what matters is that they are transformed in their way of living by their faith in Christ.

*Gospel: Matthew 7:21-27*
The awesome Sermon on the Mount, with its radical summary of Christian morality, comes to a close with these verses which focus on two dire warnings given to two different groups. In the first warning, those who would claim that they are followers of Jesus because of their interest in piety and the things of religion are dismissed from Christ's presence because they have had no real interest in doing God's will. That will has just been spoken about by Jesus in the Sermon; it means loving as the Father loves, praying for enemies, doing good to those who hate you.

The second warning is related to this because in it Jesus uses the imagery of the difference between building on sand and on rock to show who the true disciples are. If we imagine we can be true disciples by simply listening and not doing, we are merely fooling ourselves. St Matthew's Jewish background comes through here as we see the connection between the first reading and the gospel. In the Sermon, which is the new Law, Jesus is offering us a transformed way of living, but we must choose it not merely with our heads but with our hearts and hands. The alternative is to become a hypocrite and they are the people Jesus has the harshest words for in the entire gospel.

*Reflection*
It is probably true to say that in every generation great harm is done to the message of Jesus not by non-believers but by those who claim to serve it. People can become enthusiastic about certain devotions, saints, novenas and places of pilgrimage and, in their lives they may, in their religious fervour, ignore Jesus in the needy who are right there in front of them. The authenticity of our faith in Christ can never be properly measured by acts of piety or even religious fervour and that is the sobering message that comes from the scriptures today. It suits some of us to use the message of Jesus as a kind of truth that allows us to point the finger at others in a judgemental way but that is not the kind of faith Jesus asks of us. He simply asks us to remember that what we do to the least of our brothers and sisters we do also to him.

THE TENTH SUNDAY IN ORDINARY TIME

*First Reading: Hosea 6:3-6*
Themes touched upon in last week's readings are present again today and this is apparent in the very moving extract from the prophet Hosea. He prophesied some 740 years before Jesus, yet his words exercised a strong influence on his teaching and preaching as can be seen from the gospel for today. The reading is divided in two parts. In the first, God is quoting the kind of thing the Israelites might say: pious words that apparently reflect a deep faith. However, God is not impressed with their words and is tired of their periodic bouts of fervour. So in his frustration he asks: 'What am I to do with you?' He appeals to them yet again to listen to the prophets and to get it into their heads that their God is not interested in the kind of piety and

devotion that has them rushing to the temple to offer sacrifices. He is in fact only interested in the practice of covenant love that is based on peace and justice.

*Second Reading: Romans 4:18-25*
In Paul's writing, Abraham plays an important role and that is because unlike Moses he is not identified with either the giving of the Law or its observance. Abraham trusted in God and was obedient to his word before ever there was a Torah to be kept and it is for this reason that Paul makes much of Abraham's faith, a phenomenon that is referred to a great deal in Genesis and in Jewish tradition. Abraham's faith justified him before God – in other words he was considered God's friend because of it. Now the promise to Abraham that his descendants would be as many as the stars of heaven is fulfilled because in Christ the Gentiles are being justified outside the Law of Moses. They are made God's friends through their faith in Christ. The point might seem a little convoluted to us but for Paul it was essential that he should show how scripture prepared for a time when non-Jews could be considered justified even though they did not keep the Law of Moses. The point for Paul is the infinite love of God which reaches out to all peoples through Christ.

*Gospel: Matthew 9:9-13*
The story related in today's gospel shows the necessary link between words and deeds that was mentioned last week. Jesus calls Matthew, a tax collector, to follow him. While usually associated with the evangelist, scholars believe that this was a different person, a Jew of the scribal tradition who made use of Mark's gospel to write his own account of Jesus' ministry. Whatever about his identity, the point in the gospel is clear. A sinner, made so by his profession and therefore an excluded person, responds to Jesus in the same way as the first apostles (4:18-22). The scandal of the situation is compounded by the fact that Jesus then goes and has dinner with him and his friends. Sitting at table with such people rendered Jesus unclean and the Pharisees are not slow to take offence at his behaviour. Jesus' reply goes to the heart of the matter: his ministry of proclaiming the kingdom is not just about words. By all his actions Jesus

shows the true nature of God – his ministry of healing is also a reaching out to sinners. He reminds his opponents that in the scriptures which they claim to know and follow, God wants mercy not sacrifice. This is the text of today's first reading and here we see Jesus reading and interpreting the scriptures to proclaim the love of God.

*Reflection*
It's probably just as well that Jesus never engaged a publicity manager or a media consultant to help him promote his ministry. Such handlers would most likely have steered him away from the likes of Matthew and warned him never to be seen at a party in his house. However, Jesus never set out to be a people pleaser. He only wants to be faithful to God's will. Strangely, it is not always our sins that are the greatest obstacle to getting to know God better but our self righteousness. Today we are invited to ponder deeply the meaning of mercy as Jesus preached it and lived it. Such prayerful reflection will not leave us the way it found us.

## THE ELEVENTH SUNDAY IN ORDINARY TIME

*First Reading: Exodus 19:2-6*
When Moses was shepherding his father-in-law's flock in Sinai he experienced the God of his ancestors in a way that would change his life forever (Ex 3:1-16). He came to know that God cared for the plight of his oppressed people in Egypt and that he would save them and bring them to himself. It is the culmination of the fulfillment of that promise that we see in this reading. The Israelites have escaped from Pharaoh and have journeyed to the holy mountain where Moses had been a shepherd. It is here that they will come to understand that the events of the Exodus were pointers to the identity of their God Yahweh. He is the liberator who wishes to make a covenant with these refugee slaves. Until this point the covenants in the Bible had been promises on God's part such as the covenant with Noah (Gen 9:9) or with Abraham (Gen 15:1-18). Now at Sinai the people are to respond to Yahweh by living the life he asks of them and which is shown in the law which is given to Moses. Adherence to the covenant will make

81

LET THE READER UNDERSTAND

them the chosen people of God, his treasured possession. This is the cornerstone of Israelite religion and only by understanding it can we grasp the full significance of the new covenant in Christ.

## Second Reading: Romans 5:6-11

Paul's letter to the Romans was written between AD56 and 58. At the time of writing he was in Corinth but on his way to Jerusalem from where he hoped to travel to Rome and then on to Spain to continue his mission of preaching the gospel. However, as things turned out he was arrested in Jerusalem and ended up being sent to Rome as a prisoner (Acts 21:30-33). In the letter, as we have already seen, he is explaining how he understands the significance of the death and resurrection of Jesus. This reading is from chapter 5 and in the earlier chapters he has shown the dire situation of sinful humanity, lost without a true sense of God. In this section he shows how our salvation lies in Christ whose death on the cross takes away our sins. Through him we have been justified or made righteous. This is the technical vocabulary that Paul uses to illustrate how an alienated humanity is now restored to friendship with God. What has taken place is the pure gift of God and it is offered to all, both Jews and Gentiles. This is the message that fires Paul in his missionary journeys: we have not earned or deserved this wonderful grace. It is totally the work of a merciful God whose infinite love is beyond our imagining.

## Gospel: Matthew 9:36-10:8

Appropriately enough, Jesus' call of the apostles begins with his awareness of the sorry state of the people who are dejected and harassed 'like sheep without a shepherd'. This use of the imagery of shepherding is a reference to their leaders who have failed to care for them. Now Jesus wishes to call others to share in his ministry of bearing witness to the kingdom. A sense of urgency is introduced with a change of imagery to that of the harvest. The time is now and the people are ready to hear the good news, but who will proclaim it to them? These twelve 'apostles' are people sent by their master and empowered by him for their task. In terms of church history, the twelve apostles represent the authentic tradition of the church as it seeks to be faithful to the word and work of Jesus. It is striking that the group chosen for this task are such a motley crew and from a wide variety of backgrounds. They include rebels and collaborators, one who will deny Jesus, another who will betray him and others who are only interested in who should be first. And all of them will run away in the end!

*Reflection*
The events of the Exodus in which an enslaved people were freed and taught the way of covenant love were the first steps in the unfolding drama of the human race coming to understand the true nature of God. This drama would culminate in the new Exodus when Jesus would reveal to all the kingdom of God in which sins are forgiven and human beings can learn to live in love and service of one another. In choosing the twelve, he is in a way choosing us all, willing to risk himself and his message to weak human beings who will fail him and give scandal by their behaviour. Perhaps the most surprising thing is that the good news continues to be heard. If Jesus only called the perfect or those who could be depended upon to be totally committed to their task, what would we be left with? A church of the elite! However, Jesus came to call sinners and that's the reason that we know he is calling us.

## THE TWELFTH SUNDAY IN ORDINARY TIME

*First Reading: Jeremiah 20:10-13*
The prophet Jeremiah preached in Jerusalem in the period before the destruction of the city and its temple in the year 587. His message was an unpopular one because he told the people that it was useless for them to live the way they were living and still expect God to come and save them just because they dwelt in the holy city. He attacked them for their breaches of the covenant, for their treatment of the poor and for their stubborn refusal to recognise what was going on around them. This brought him into conflict with his contemporaries and we find evidence of his struggle with them at various points in the book. Chapter 20 is one such case and in this reading the prophet is reporting what they are saying about him. On this occasion he turns confidently

83

to the Lord to ask his help and he expresses his prayer in a way which does not sit too easily with Christian perspective when he asks God to let him see the vengeance he will take on them. The point here is not so much that he wants to see his enemies punished as that he needs to know that God is with him in his difficulties. In the gospel for today, this theme is echoed when Jesus warns his followers that they will be persecuted but he calls on them to persevere.

*Second Reading: Romans 5:12-15*
We continue to read from chapter 5 in which Paul is explaining what has taken place in Christ, and at this point he decides to make a comparison that contrasts the effects of Adam's sin with the salvation won for us by Jesus. Adam is the first man and as such is a type of every man. He is not so much blaming Adam for all sin as saying that just as he sinned so do we all. He stresses that the consequence of sin is death and by this he is referring first and foremost to the death of our friendship with God. So if it is true that because of one man we have lost our way to God how much more true is it that by one man, Christ, the second Adam, all may now find their way back to God? Indeed, for Paul, what Christ has won for us is far greater than what was lost through Adam, for in him we have come to share in the very life of God through the gift of the Holy Spirit.

*Gospel: Matthew 10:20-31*
Having called the twelve, Jesus now instructs them for the task and times that lie ahead. The proclamation of the kingdom, which begins in Jesus, will only be properly understood in the light of the resurrection and then the apostles will be at the forefront of bringing this good news to the whole world. However, they must understand from the outset that there is a price to be paid. If Jesus was persecuted so too will they be but his repeated appeal to them in this passage is: 'Do not be afraid.' Their lack of fear is to be based on their knowledge of God's abiding love of them in all circumstances and this will see them through the toughest of times. There is of course a challenge in this: no-one can be a secret Christian in the sense of just for him or her self. We are to declare for Christ in public and be prepared for the

consequences. In the early church there were times when this resulted in persecution and even martyrdom, and so the challenging aspect of these words would have been very clear to those
who first read them.

*Reflection*
Paul and Jeremiah were both Jews, separated by 600 years of
turbulent history, yet the distance between them in their understanding of God could only be measured in light years. Even
though Jeremiah was utterly convinced of the faithfulness of
God, he could never have imagined that his mercy towards a
sinful humanity would be manifested in the way which Paul
proclaimed. In the person of his Son it is as though God recreates
us, we have a new Adam who shows us how to live as God
wants. Every person is given a unique dignity as a child of God.
Let us strive to become more and more aware of what this
means for the way we live and how we treat one another.

THE THIRTEENTH SUNDAY IN ORDINARY TIME

*First Reading: 2 Kings 4:8-11, 14-1*
The prophet Elisha was the successor to Elijah and the stories
about both men and their exploits are to be found at the end of
the first book of Kings and the beginning of the second. In this
brief extract we are told about the woman who showed hospital-
ity to the prophet as he went on his travels through Israel. Since
he visited on a number of occasions, she decided that they
should use their resources to offer him some comfort. When
Elisha discovers what she has done he asks his servant what
they might do for her and he is informed that she has no children and her husband is old. So he calls the woman and tells her
that within the year she would have a son and indeed it comes to
pass. The theme of the barren woman conceiving is one found
often in the Old Testament and it emphasises God's care for
those on the margins, for such women would have been considered cursed by their contemporaries. In this story, her welcome
for the man of God was similar to welcoming God himself and
such an attitude brings forth life.

In the gospel for today Jesus promises blessings for those who would offer even a cup of water to his disciples, for in welcoming them we welcome Jesus and the Father who sent him.

*Second Reading: Romans 6:3-4, 8-11*
We have already seen in Romans how Paul uses the words life and death to refer to more than our physical existence and its termination. He wants us to understand that being alive is about being alive to God, being aware that our whole existence only has its true meaning when it is rooted in this fact. By the same token death is not simply the end of our mortal existence – rather it means being cut off from God and this may be how we are, even though we are still alive physically. Paul employs this imagery in today's reading to help us understand the central role of baptism. Our baptism is a metaphorical death. It is as though when we are going down into the water we are going into the tomb with Jesus. Then, just as Christ rose from the tomb, so too we rise with him to a new life in God. This life is no longer dominated by sin but by our relationship with Jesus.

*Gospel: Matthew 10:37-42*
These verses conclude Jesus' words to the apostles about their mission. He informs them again about the difficulties that will lie ahead but in the midst of persecution and rejection they will know that the Lord is with them. This is why Jesus says that nothing else, no other loyalty or affection, should have a greater claim on us than our decision to follow Jesus. The paradox of the gospel is clearly presented: we will truly live only if we die to ourselves. Jesus goes on to say that whoever receives one of his followers because of their allegiance to him will be rewarded. This is true no matter what the status of the follower, one of the leaders or one of the 'little ones'. The staggering point made here by Jesus is reflected in the theme of the first reading. When we care for the one in need we care for the Lord himself.

*Reflection*
If we were asked to explain to someone who had never heard of Christianity what it is, how would we go about it? It is a ques-

tion worth pondering because our answer will tell us a lot about ourselves and whether or not we see it as anything more than a set of moral guidelines given to us by God to enable us to get to heaven. For St Paul, it was certainly much more than that and this was because he understood that Christianity is about a relationship which transforms us from within. It is a dynamic coming to life, a growing into an awareness of just how much we are loved by God. If we grasp this, then we can learn to see the face of God in those around us and to respond to his presence, not just in the obviously holy or sacred but also in the mundane and ordinary.

## The Fourteenth Sunday in Ordinary Time

*First Reading: Zechariah 9:9-10*
The book of the prophet Zechariah originates in the period after the Israelites' return from exile (ca 500). Indeed many commentators believe that there are in fact two books made up of chapters 1-8 and 9-14. One of the most striking features of this work is the use of visions to show the prophet what is taking place (1:8). An angel then explains these visions and in this process we have the beginning of apocalyptic writing. The best known example of it in the Old Testament is in Daniel 7-12 and, of course, in the New Testament it is found in the book of Revelation. In our reading for today the Jewish people are presented with an image of the king God will send them. At this period in their history they have no kings and are looking forward to a time when the Lord's anointed (i.e. Messiah) would come and free them. The vision offered here is not of a mighty military leader astride a war-horse but of a humble king sitting on an ass. He will bring peace not only to Israel (Ephraim is another name for the Israelites) but to the whole world. It is this vision which explains the significance of Jesus' triumphal entry into Jerusalem on a donkey.

*Second Reading: Romans 8:9,11-13*
We have already noted how Paul makes much use of contrasting ideas to bring home his message. Once again in this reading he talks about life and death, the spiritual and the unspiritual. In so

doing he is trying to emphasise both the unique gift that Christianity is and the tremendous opportunity it offers for transformation in the life of the believer. In the extract we are reading today, Paul is making much of the difference between living spiritually or unspiritually. In the latter case, we are focused in on ourselves and relying on purely human strength. The alternative is to be turned towards Christ and relying on the power which comes from God. Such spiritual living is possible only because we possess the Spirit of Christ. This is the very Spirit which raised Jesus from death and which gives life to us in the here and now.

*Gospel: Matthew 11:25-30*
Jesus was very aware that faith in God should be a life giving force for those who believe but he was equally aware that religion can be a force that oppresses people. Some of his contemporaries claimed that observance of the 613 commandments of the law was the way to life and they called it taking upon oneself the 'yoke of the kingdom of God'. These people, the scribes and Pharisees, were opposed to much of what Jesus was doing but at the same time many others heard him gladly. These were people who were forced out by a system that could only condemn them as sinners. Now in these verses, Jesus utters a beautiful prayer of thanksgiving to God for what is taking place: those in most need of the good news are coming to know God's love for them. In inviting the weary and overburdened to come to him he offers them a yoke not of more and more rules but of a relationship, in which the gentle and humble love of the Saviour allows them to find their dignity as children of God.

*Reflection*
Today's readings are an invitation to focus on what it is that we really want. At the time of the prophet the people longed for someone who would bring them victory by destroying their enemies, and God offered them a servant king who would bring them peace. In Paul, the choice is put even more starkly: do you want to live for yourselves trapped in your own selfishness or do you want to turn outwards to God and be truly free? In the gospel for today Jesus helps us to answer when he says: 'Come

to me all you who labour and are heavily burdened.' The rest he offers is not to be confused with some kind of otherworldly detachment; it is a way to engage with the world that we live in, seeing it through God's eyes.

*First Reading: Isaiah 55:10-11*
As we have noted before, the Book of the Prophet Isaiah does not all come from the time of the prophet in the eighth century. The section from 40-55, sometimes known as Second Isaiah, stems from the period towards the end of Israel's exile in Babylon (around 540BC). These chapters are an encouragement to the exiles to hope again in Yahweh their God, for they will soon have the opportunity to return home. In chapter 55 God is offering them again the chance to experience his presence with them and is inviting them to put their trust in his word. Today's short reading helps us to understand the whole notion of the Word of God as it was understood in the Old Testament. It was not simply a command to be obeyed, or even a spoken word that could be heard. It was the revelation of God's saving will for his people in all the circumstances of their lives. In these verses, the simple image of rain is used to show how God's word has a fruitful purpose which it always fulfils.

*Second Reading: Romans 8:18-23*
In this reading Paul is continuing to tease out the implications of the death and resurrection of Christ. The gift of the Spirit means that we are brought into union with God in a way we never would have imagined but, even more than that, the entire creation is drawn into the saving plan of God. The alienation of sin, which has stopped human beings reaching their full potential, has also impeded the created order from fulfilling its destiny, but now it too will share in the redemption which has been won for us by Christ. This too is a work of the Spirit and what Paul is saying stresses the biblical view that creation in its entirety is good and from God. This goes against some of the philosophies of his time which would have considered anything to do with the material world as being inferior or even evil.

*Gospel: Matthew 13:1-23*

This chapter on parables follows on from Jesus' conflicts with the religious leaders of his time. While their teaching was dominated by appeals to oral tradition and authorities from the past, Jesus' teaching was characterised by his use of parables. Parables have been usefully defined as 'short stories with a double meaning' and through these Jesus, using images and metaphors that were part of people's everyday lives, invited them to think deeply about the ways of God. In the parable today Jesus relates a simple scene of someone sowing seed. This would have been a common sight and a regular part of the life experience of his Galilean audience. As Jesus tells it, nothing extraordinary happens and yet through this imagery he invites them to reflect on their experience and see what it might say to them about where and how God is at work in their lives and how they are responding to him. The basic metaphor here is one of growth or the lack of it and it is a symbol of Jesus' own ministry of preaching the kingdom. Some never give him a chance, others are enthusiastic but not prepared for the long haul, and others become derailed by the worries of the world or material concerns. Finally, those who hear the word and take it to heart bear fruit in staggering quantities, way beyond what any farmer might reasonably expect. The point is that the kingdom preached by Jesus is both a gift and a challenge. What happens to the fruitful word that is sown is up to us.

*Reflection*

All the parables of Jesus are an invitation to reflection and a reminder that the Christian life cannot be lived on 'auto-pilot'. Today Jesus asks us how good our hearing is and it could happen that we don't hear the question because we are too concerned about other things. We have many worries and the pressures of modern living appear to be at a far remove from the gentle image of a farmer going out to sow. However, the human condition is the same now as then and Jesus is still challenging us to think about how we receive his still fruitful word. It is a reminder that we must not only talk to God but also listen as well.

## THE SIXTEENTH SUNDAY IN ORDINARY TIME

*First Reading: Wisdom 12:13, 16-19*
The Book of Wisdom is the last book of the Old Testament to be written, possibly composed some 60 years before the birth of Jesus. It was written in Greek and was intended for well-educated Jews who were living in a pagan environment. Its author wanted them to see that their faith could stand up to the critique levelled at it by pagan philosophers. In the last part of the book from which we are reading today, the author wishes to show how God's wisdom is to be seen in the history of his dealings with the Israelites, especially in the great event of the exodus. He emphasises that the power of God is not only to be seen in mighty deeds such as the dividing of the waters but also in the exercise of his mercy. This in turn teaches a lesson to humankind that they too should deal in a kindly way with each other. The power of God is not merely exercised to show how powerful God is but rather with a view to showing how God cares for everything he has made.

*Second Reading: Romans 8:26-27*
Earlier in chapter 8 Paul has highlighted that the gift of the Spirit makes us true children of God and enables us to cry out 'Abba, Father' which was the very prayer of Jesus in Gethsemane (v 15). In today's short but enormously significant reading, we see the consequences of the indwelling of the Spirit for Christian prayer. The New Testament is consistently clear on the importance of prayer for the life of the believer. Paul himself goes so far as to say that we should pray constantly (Rom12:12) and a clue as to just how that might be possible is given in his understanding of the Spirit praying within us. As finite and weak human beings, prayer can be difficult for us but Paul encourages us to hand over our struggles in prayer to the Spirit who prays in our hearts. We can be confident that God who knows what is in our hearts knows well what the Spirit means.

*Gospel: Matthew 13:24-43*
We have parables again this Sunday, no less than three and they are all about growth but each from a different perspective. If we

still think of the kingdom of God as referring to the afterlife then reflecting on these short stories will help us to think differently.

The first parable of the weeds and the wheat tells an unusual story of someone trying to sabotage a good harvest; the second focuses on the tiny mustard seed and the change it undergoes, while the third moves away from farming to the kitchen and the importance of a little yeast in making the bread rise. Each of these parables presents important points for reflection about the ways of God in the world. The first one challenges us to recognise that sometimes we must learn to live with certain situations we don't like because the effort to remove or change them would do more harm than good. In the second, we are asked to remember that God often works in small and apparently insignificant ways to bring about great change. Finally, the yeast is mixed right through the flour and is no longer identifiable but it is there and it works, so too the ways of God are mixed in through all the daily experiences and can achieve their results without us knowing how.

*Reflection*
Saint Bernard of Clairvaux was a great theologian and he coined the phrase: 'The greatest enemy of the good is the perfect.' Sometimes the good we do is lost because of an endless striving after a perfection that is not attainable. There is a tension for those who follow the gospel between giving of our best and being aware of our limitations. Undoubtedly Jesus wants us to give of our best but there is much over which we have no control. Our contribution may at times seem small like a mustard seed but it can grow in ways we do not imagine. Like the leaven in the flour the small bit of good we do may have consequences way beyond our understanding. When it comes to the kingdom of God we move in faith, faith in a God of surprises who won't allow any effort to be wasted but who also wants us to trust that things are unfolding as they should.

*First Reading: 1 Kings 3:5, 7-12*
In this reading from the First Book of Kings, we are brought to the beginning of the reign of Solomon which was around 940BC. After the death of David, Solomon became king in Israel and inherited a country that was finally at peace. Yet the young man had much to learn and what we see today is that he was aware of his need. So when God asks him what he would like, he immediately asks for what he needs to be a good king and that is a discerning heart. Since his prayer is not a selfish one, God hears and answers him and thus begins the long tradition in the Bible regarding the wisdom of Solomon. In the Old Testament wisdom plays a very important part in the growing relationship between the Israelites and their God for through it they learn to seek what is really important and to put everything else in perspective. It is that same tradition which is alluded to in the parables told by Jesus in the gospel for today.

*Second Reading: Romans 8:28-30*
As we continue our reading from chapter 8, we see yet another consequence of the presence and activity of the Spirit in the life of the believer. Having just spoken of the role of the Spirit in prayer, Paul goes on now to show that no matter what happens to us God can and does turn it to the good. He explains that the plan which is unfolding now has been there since the beginning. That is to say that we are called to become like Jesus, sharing in his destiny. Just as his Son endured the cross and now shares in the glory of the Father, so too all the faithful are called by God to share in friendship with him (to be justified) and to participate in the glory which is his. It is not easy to see how everything that happens to us can be for our good, and indeed sometimes the phrase 'it is God's will' can be used in a way which suggests that God somehow wants terrible things to happen to people. Nothing could be further from the truth! St Paul wants us to understand that even though we may have to undergo great difficulties, God is there with us and that good can and does come from it.

*Gospel: Matthew 13:44-52*
We come now to the last three parables of chapter 13 and, as before, they focus on the kingdom of God. It is interesting that Jesus never offered a theological definition of this central theme in his preaching, he simply kept telling stories to illustrate various aspects of it. In the parables told today the emphasis is on how we should respond to the mystery of God's kingdom in the world around us. In the first parable, someone finds a treasure they were not even looking for; rather in their daily toil they come across it. They recognise it for what it is and realise that they must do everything necessary to take possession of it. Even though there is upheaval it does not compare with the joy the finder experiences. The second story has a similar theme only this time the person is in search of and finds the pearl of great price and once again everything else must be abandoned as he takes the necessary steps to buy the pearl. The concluding story is different and deals with two aspects of the mystery of the kingdom that we have already mentioned: it is both a gift and a challenge. The net thrown into the sea catches fish of every kind – meaning that the invitation to the kingdom is universal. Yet there is a process of sorting because we must choose the ways of the kingdom; it contains an element of judgement, for each one must be accountable for their actions.

*Reflection*
Over the last few weeks we have heard a selection of parables that invite us to take time and think about the topic that most characterised the preaching of Jesus: the kingdom of God. We would do well now to ask ourselves how we see it unfolding in our own lives? Where do we recognise the gift of God in what is happening to us at this time? Also, where is the room for growth and how is God challenging me to be a better disciple? Perhaps most importantly of all, we need to give thanks for the invitation to be a part of this wonderful plan of God that is unfolding in so many ways and is at one and the same time dependent on my response and yet still fruitful in spite of me.

## THE EIGHTEENTH SUNDAY IN ORDINARY TIME

*First Reading: Isaiah 55:1-3*
The section of the Book of the Prophet Isaiah from which this text is taken probably dates from the time of the exile when the Jewish people had been driven from their homes by the Babylonians. It was a time of great calamity for the Jews as they felt that God, whose presence was assured by the gift of the Promised Land and by the temple in Jerusalem, was now no longer with them since they now had neither temple nor land. Into this situation of despair come these words of hope and en-couragement. Using imagery of want as experienced through hunger, thirst and poverty, the prophet tells them that their deepest need, which is for God, will be generously met. They only have to turn away from themselves and to look towards their Lord and their soul will live. For the person of faith, it is God's word that gives true nourishment and in this text it is God himself who urgently pleads with his people to listen to him.

*Second Reading: Romans 8:35, 37-39*
As we have already seen, Paul has been explaining the meaning of faith in Christ through an emphasis on our being joined to the risen Jesus through baptism. The verses we read today represent the highpoint of his teaching as he presents in the most stirring language the significance of what God has done for us through the death and resurrection of his Son. All that has happened is to be understood as an act of overwhelming love and, no matter what our circumstances, there is nothing which can separate us from that love. In order to drive that point home Paul insists that there is nothing in the entire created order which can come be-tween us and the love of God made visible in Christ Jesus our Lord. This is indeed the Christian gospel, the good news!

*Gospel: Matthew 14:13-21*
The story of the multiplication of the loaves and fishes is the only miracle of Jesus that is recounted in all four gospels. In Matthew's account we see different aspects of the ministry of Jesus as he responds to different situations. The scene is set with news of the execution of John the Baptist reaching Jesus and his

response is to want to take some time out, but that was not to be as the people headed after him in their thousands. His response to this is one of compassion and he sets about healing the sick among them. The disciples do not want to be responsible for such a crowd so at day's end they wish to send them away. Jesus, on the other hand, wants to nourish them and using language that echoes the practice of the Eucharist Jesus blesses the bread that will satisfy their hunger.

*Reflection*
Reading texts such as those put before us today, it is hard to understand why it is that so many people have a faith which is based on fear, or on an idea of God that is somehow threatening or judgemental. Perhaps it is because we suspect that this is too good to be true, that there must a catch. We project on to God our conditional, human way of loving and so we can satisfy ourselves as to the limits of his love. Today's readings are yet another wonderful opportunity for us to take the risk of really hearing what it is that God is saying to us. Jesus reveals the God who is full of compassion, who heals our ills and who nourishes us. Let us put ourselves into his hands once again.

THE NINETEENTH SUNDAY IN ORDINARY TIME

*First Reading: 1 Kings 19:9, 11-13*
The background to this reading, which helps us to understand its full meaning, is that the prophet Elijah has fled from the land of Israel, fearful for his life. King Ahab and Queen Jezebel want him dead because he is undermining their rule in the country by challenging the idolatry which they have introduced. He flees to Horeb, which is another name for Mt Sinai where the Israelites first entered into a covenant with Yahweh. On that occasion it was in the midst of awesome signs, on the quaking mountain, that God was revealed to them through his servant Moses (Ex19-20). By contrast, this time the frightened and dejected prophet meets God not in the spectacular or the miraculous but rather in the gentle silence of the breeze. On recognising the presence of God, he covers his face in an act of reverence and then is called once again by the Lord to return to Israel and continue his mission of proclaiming the word.

## Second Reading: Romans 9:1-5

Having extolled the wonders that Christ has accomplished for those who turn to him, Paul now turns his attention to what is for him a very painful issue. Over the next three chapters he will concern himself with how it is that the Jewish leaders have failed to recognise Jesus as the Messiah. Sometimes, in our emphasis on his conversion, we can forget that Paul remained a Jew and stayed faithful to the religion of his ancestors. His dramatic insight was that the good news was not just for Jews but for Gentiles as well. In today's reading we get some glimpse of the depth of his feeling for his 'own flesh and blood' when he says he would even be prepared to be cut off from Christ if he thought it would help his people. After all, as he says, it is 'from their flesh and blood came Christ who is above all God forever blessed!'

## Gospel: Matthew 14:22-33

Following on from the feeding of the five thousand, Jesus sends away both the disciples and the crowds and then goes off to pray. He then comes to meet the disciples who are in a boat on the lake and battling a strong headwind. As he comes to them walking on the water their response is one of fear, a fear which Jesus tries to allay. Peter wants to believe it is the Lord and so asks to be invited to come to him across the water. It is only when his focus goes from Jesus that he feels the force of the wind and begins to sink. Jesus reaches out and saves him and at the same time rebukes him for his lack of faith.

The scene ends with them all in the boat, calm has descended and the disciples are worshipping their Lord and Master. The imagery here invites reflection on what it means to belong to a community of faith as well as to be an individual believer. Through life's storms we will certainly experience times of doubt and fear but this should not disappoint us – rather we need to be in the habit of paying attention to the Lord's presence as one who will always guide us safely to shore.

## Reflection

Hero worship can be a dangerous thing for we can easily forget that our heroes have feet of clay. This is also true in the realm of faith, where our idea of the saints removes them from the ordinary pains and struggles of human existence. Our readings today present us with three great people of prayer and action who still experienced disappointment, doubt and frustration. This realisation about the mighty Elijah, Paul and Peter, far from demeaning them, reminds us that the journey of faith is never one in which we have all the answers. Indeed, it is often one in which we can only take God's hand and go forward in trust.

## THE TWENTIETH SUNDAY IN ORDINARY TIME

*First Reading: Isaiah 56:1, 6-7*
An important theme developed in the Old Testament, and seen especially in the writings of some of the prophets, is that of universalism. In other words, the God of the Israelites gradually reveals that his concern is not only for one race or ethnic group but for all the nations of the world. This trend can be seen in today's first reading. Taken from the last part of the book of Isaiah, which dates from around 500BC, these verses indicate God's desire to save everyone and may in their time have caused some resentment among those who had suffered at the hands of the Babylonians and other empires that had conquered Israel. Nonetheless, God's intention is clear: anyone who respects the demands of the covenant will be welcome in God's house.

*Second Reading: Romans 11:13-15, 29-32*
This reading continues with Paul's attempts to explain why God has allowed his chosen people to reject Jesus. Addressing the Gentiles, he tells them that his work among them might cause some of his own people to be jealous and make them think again about their attitude to Jesus. He is clearly hoping that, as the Gentiles were once considered beyond the plan of God but are now very much included, so the Jews might one day rejoice in the grace of Christ. Paul's arguments are those of a man who feels this dilemma very deeply but who does not know exactly what is taking place, and who longs for reconciliation between Jews and Christians.

*Gospel: Matthew 15:21-28*

For those who are used to the idea of 'gentle Jesus, meek and mild' this reading comes as something of a shock. The incident takes place outside the territory of the Jews to where, we are told, Jesus has withdrawn. A Canaanite woman approaches Jesus and the use of this word to describe her immediately tells us there might be a problem here. The Canaanites were the traditional enemies of the Israelites in the Old Testament, but the word would not have been in use at the time of Jesus. The problem that arises, however, is not because of anything the woman says or does, indeed readers would be surprised at her calling out to Jesus using titles such as Lord and Son of David. Foreigner she may be, but she is aware of Jesus' identity and approaches him in faith. However, it is only her persistence and the embarrassment of the disciples that earns her a hearing. Jesus explains that his mission is first and foremost to the Jewish people, that the children's food cannot be given to house dogs. This rebuff still does not deter her and Jesus is finally struck by the faith of this outsider and grants her request for the healing of her daughter. In these days of political correctness, the words of Jesus could be taken as offensive but the point of the story in its own time was to emphasise that it is a deep personal faith in Jesus as Messiah that can bring about the salvation we seek, no matter who were are or where we are from.

*Reflection*

The readings today have some surprises that may be lost on modern hearers because we are not sufficiently aware of the religious and ethnic tensions that lie behind them. However, many would be surprised at the response of Jesus and it is important to take time to deal with that. We are presented here with a Jesus who at first sight appears to be unwilling to help, but we are also presented with a Jesus who can be reached and indeed forced into a change of heart. This is Jesus the man who also had to learn about the universal will of his Father to save all people. He was taught this lesson not in a theology class but through an encounter with a human being in need, and Matthew's Jewish-Christian community held on to this memory because they too had to come to terms with welcoming outsiders into their midst.

There are many lessons for today's world, plagued as it is by all kinds of fundamentalisms, in this encounter between Jesus and the unnamed foreign woman.

THE TWENTY-FIRST SUNDAY IN ORDINARY TIME

*First Reading: Isaiah 22:19-23*
This unusual passage from Isaiah refers to an incident during the life of the prophet when an important official at the royal court, by the name of Shebna, was demoted from office. The one who took his place as Master of the Palace is given full authority over the royal household. It is clear from the text that this was a very important and prestigious position and this is demonstrated by the ritual of handing over the key as a symbol of his authority. As holder of the key Eliakim has control over access to the king. The choice of this passage is directly related to today's gospel and helps us to understand it. In Mt 16:13-20 Peter acknowledges that Jesus is indeed the Christ. In response to his confession of faith, Jesus confirms him as leader of the twelve, the rock upon whom the church is built and the one who receives the keys of the kingdom. As is made clear in the rest of the gospel, Peter's authority is based on service.

*Second Reading: Romans 11:33-36*
These verses which are a short hymn of praise bring to a conclusion that section of the letter to the Romans in which Paul has struggled to explain how it is that his own people, the Jews, have failed to recognise Jesus as the Messiah. He has reasoned that in the providence of God it was the Jewish rejection of Jesus which meant that the message was brought to the Gentiles. Now Paul awaits the time when the conversion of the Gentiles to the ways of God will in turn be a cause for the Jews to accept Jesus.

This reasoning leads him into a reflection on the wisdom of God which is away beyond anything that the human mind can grasp. However, his reflection does not lead him to a sense of frustration but to an outpouring of praise and thanksgiving to the eternal God who holds all things in being.

*Gospel: Matthew 16:13-20*

The central question of faith in Jesus that was addressed in last week's gospel is once again to the fore, but it is Peter who is centre stage this time. In asking the question about his identity, Jesus opens the way for all the possible ideas to be mentioned and the replies reflect the fact that among the Jews of the time there were a variety of expectations about their religious future and what it might bring. However, in calling himself the Son of Man the ground is prepared for Peter's answer. In the Book of Daniel this expression is used to describe a messiah-like figure in one of the visions (7:13). By the time of the New Testament it was a way for the early church to speak about Jesus as God's anointed one.

Peter's full reply marks him out as one blessed by God with insight and so he is given his leadership role. However, as we shall soon see, Peter still has much to learn both about himself and about leadership in the church.

*Reflection*

In a certain sense, the first two readings help us understand what is taking place in the gospel for today. In Isaiah we see the connection between the imagery of the keys and the importance of what is being said to Peter. Then like Paul, we can wonder at how things have turned out and why it is that God has given such a vital role to frail human beings. Let it be a cause of wonder to us that God in his wisdom has allowed such a rich treasure as the gospel to be held in 'earthen vessels'. After two thousand years, and despite its many failings, the church still proclaims the good news, not depending on itself but guided by the wisdom of God.

THE TWENTY-SECOND SUNDAY IN ORDINARY TIME

*First Reading: Jeremiah 20:7-9*

We rarely receive insights into the personal struggles of the prophets in the Bible but today we are treated to a remarkable 'confession' from the prophet Jeremiah. His ministry spanned the period leading up to the destruction of Jerusalem by the

LET THE READER UNDERSTAND

Babylonians. He could say what lay ahead for the Israelites and warned them constantly that they were treading a dangerous path. However, all he received for his efforts was 'insult and derision' and in today's reading we see how he has tried to put aside his work and just forget all about the name of God. He likens God to a lover who has seduced him. He wants to escape from the relationship but he cannot, for God's word is like a fire within and he is weary with the effort of holding it in. It is a very moving passage which, when combined with 15:10-21, allows us to see Jeremiah as a man who suffered much on account of his faith in Yahweh and yet he was prepared to speak the message in season and out of season.

*Second Reading: Romans 12:1-2*
We come now to the last section of the letter to the Romans. As is usual for Paul, the last part of an epistle is devoted to encouraging words, offering practical advice for living the Christian life. In this short reading Paul is exhorting the Christians in Rome, who were of both Jewish and pagan backgrounds, to see their whole lives as a living sacrifice in which all that they do is being offered to God in prayer. The image of offering sacrifice was a powerful one in the ancient world for both Jews and Gentiles. This was something undertaken regularly in pagan shrines and in the temple in Jerusalem. Yet Paul has a whole new understanding of sacrifice in the light of Christ. It is not so much about formal ritual in holy places on certain days. It is rather to do with transforming one's way of life from within and being modeled on the person of Christ.

*Gospel: Matthew 16:21-27*
Peter is again at the centre of things in this week's gospel but for all the wrong reasons. Jesus, having brought his followers to the point where they could say that he is the long awaited Messiah, now begins the difficult task of trying to teach them about the nature of his messiahship, and once again their preconceived notions about God, religion and salvation are going to be turned on their heads. In predicting the events of his passion and death, Jesus is making a connection between himself and the prophets of old who suffered for their fidelity to their mission, but the

idea that God's messiah might suffer at all is simply not on the cards for the disciples and Peter no doubt speaks for all present when he rejects the idea. In Jesus' temptation in the desert, Satan tried to divert Jesus from the path of true sonship. Now Peter does the same and is called Satan. Jesus explains that being a disciple means being prepared to shoulder the cross, a metaphor for suffering for what you believe in. The kingdom preached by Jesus poses a threat and so he suffers for his faithfulness to it. The same will be true for his followers.

*Reflection*

Jeremiah's suffering on account of God's word points the way to the word of the cross which Jesus speaks in the gospel for today. To embrace Christianity is to die to oneself and this is the sacrifice we are asked to make on a daily basis. The reason is not that God wants us to suffer but that the path of love which the gospel entails is one which leads us away from ourselves and that is always painful. Unlike Jeremiah we have Jesus, the Son of God, as our model on this journey. Not only does he show us the way, he walks the way with us.

THE TWENTY-THIRD SUNDAY IN ORDINARY TIME

*First Reading: Ezekiel 33:7-9*

The prophet Ezekiel was a priest of the Jerusalem temple at the time when the Babylonian armies captured the city, destroyed the temple and sent the people into exile (around 587BC). Indeed he was one of those exiled and his writing is very much a reflection of the situation in which he found himself. He pulls no punches when pointing out to the people their own responsibility for what has befallen them, but he also is at pains to emphasise the faithfulness of God. In today's extract the prophet makes use of an image with which the people would have been very familiar. God likens Ezekiel's role to that of a sentry who had the very important task of warning the people of the approach of danger. It is not enough for the prophet to save himself, he must point out the sins of the community and if he fails to do this God will hold him answerable. Jesus then takes up this idea of brotherly correction in the gospel for today where it is stressed that the

LET THE READER UNDERSTAND

community has a role to play in bringing those who stray back into the fold.

*Second Reading: Romans 13:8-10*
We continue our reading from the final section of Romans where Paul is exhorting the Christian community to live out the consequences of their faith. In today's short reading he sums up the Ten Commandments of the Old Testament in another phrase from the Old Testament which is 'love your neighbour as yourself' (Lev 19:18). With these words he goes to the heart of the gospel message and cuts through all the other obligations of the Bible. However, he is not simply restating an old command. He is showing that, because of Jesus, it now has renewed force for we have been shown how to love our neighbour by everything that Jesus said and did.

*Gospel: Matthew 18:15-20*
Chapter 18 of Matthew's gospel is devoted to relationships within the community and the first verses are concerned with the importance of not giving scandal to the weaker members of the community and ensuring that no-one is driven away because of the bad behaviour of others. In the section for today, the emphasis moves to dealing with the person who has sinned and is still part of the community. The tone of the advice is very pastoral, showing concern for everyone involved. It is only as a last resort that a decision should be taken to excommunicate anyone. There is a certain irony in the language here for they are told to treat the offender like a tax collector or sinner. In Jesus' ministry these are the people to whom he has consistently reached out. The basis for every decision the community takes must be the conviction that Christ is with them when they gather, even if only two or three of them are present. This is in contrast to the teaching of the rabbis that requires that ten men be present before the prayers can begin.

*Reflection*
The community Matthew wrote for nearly two thousand years ago bears little resemblance to the parishes where Catholics

gather for Eucharist every Sunday. So what can we learn from the type of advice given today? Firstly, our identity as a community comes from our belonging to Christ and so we wish only to act in his name. This means more than invoking his name in prayer. It means that our prayer and action should reflect his. We must not only be aware of our rights as members of the church but also of our responsibilities, especially towards those who are most at risk. For, as Paul says, 'Love is the one thing that cannot hurt your neighbour.'

THE TWENTY-FOURTH SUNDAY IN ORDINARY TIME

*First Reading: Sirach 27:33-28:9*
The Book of Sirach, which is also known as the book of Ecclesiasticus, is one of the latest books of the Old Testament, written around 190BC. It belongs to the wisdom tradition of the Bible and attempts to show how anyone who is searching for wisdom can find it in the Law of Moses. Much of the book is given over to reflecting on human behaviour and relationships and the text we read today is a good example of this. The author, who was a Jewish scribe, points out that holding onto resentment and anger can only to lead to more difficulties. This insight, which has a remarkably modern ring to it, was taken even further in the teaching of Jesus whose stress on complete forgiveness was considered very radical and challenging. For those who imagine that the Old Testament only teaches 'an eye for and eye ...', the advice given here will come as something of a surprise for not only does it encourage forgiveness but also makes the link between our willingness to forgive and our own sins being forgiven. This is exactly the point made by Jesus in the Our Father.

*Second Reading: Romans 14:7-9*
This short reading is the last in the series from the letter to the Romans and it is entirely appropriate that we should finish with these three verses, for they sum up Paul's whole outlook on Christian living. His point is that whether we live or die we belong to the Lord and so our lives should reflect this. Our entire existence is viewed from the perspective of the death and resur-

105

rection of Jesus for it is this mystery that gives meaning and purpose to how we live and indeed how we die. Our belonging to God then determines how we relate to each other and, just as it is God's love which holds the whole universe in being, so too we must be directed by that love in all our actions.

*Gospel: Matthew 18:21-35*
The community theme in chapter 18 continues this week with particular attention being given to forgiveness. Peter, perhaps as leader, makes the generous suggestion that we should be willing to forgive a person who keeps offending us as many as seven times. This was indeed generous, as among the rabbis of the time it was thought that three was a sufficient number. Jesus in his reply shows that the problem lies with the attitude behind the question. It is an attitude that fails to understand that forgiveness has its roots in the infinite love of God and because God does not stop forgiving then neither can we. To make the point effectively we are treated to a parable that offers a ridiculous scenario. It is inconceivable that a servant would owe ten thousand talents to the king. The sum is equivalent to billions of euro and such a debt could never be repaid by someone languishing in jail! However, the story drives home the contrast between the attitudes to forgiveness. We cannot expect to be forgiven and then turn around and refuse to forgive.

*Reflection*
While everybody can agree that loving your neighbour is a good thing to do, it is only when we come to specifics that we realise how difficult it can be. The ability to forgive is probably the greatest evidence of the presence of Christian love, for it is not something that we can be commanded to do. It must come from within and is evidence that the Spirit of Jesus lives in us. Letting go of hurts and resentments can be hard work but holding on to them is even more demanding for it keeps us from being at peace with ourselves and knowing our own inestimable value in the sight of God.

## THE TWENTY-FIFTH SUNDAY IN ORDINARY TIME

*First Reading: Isaiah 55:6-9*
The context for these inspiring words from Isaiah is the invit-ation from God for all who wish to come to him for abundant new life. This is against the background of the exiles returning from Babylonia to make a new start in Jerusalem. Many are keenly aware that it was the sinfulness of their own people that led to their downfall and are wondering is there any possibility of a new covenant relationship with God. Chapter 55 of Isaiah is the answer to their question. In particular, the verses we read today show how human beings must not project their own limit-ations onto God. For, while we may be lacking in forgiveness, God is infinite in mercy. So when the prophet proclaims that the heavens are as high above the earth as God's ways are above human ways, it is not to be taken as a statement about the myste-rious nature of God's actions. It is an acknowledgement that God's capacity for mercy and compassion are beyond our un-derstanding and far exceeds any human ideas about fair play. The point is brought home very forcefully in the parable Jesus tells in today's gospel.

*Second Reading: Philippians 1:20-24, 27*
It is not known when exactly Paul wrote this letter but what is obvious is that it was written while he was in prison facing a possible death sentence. This suggests to some that it was writ-ten when Paul was in Rome awaiting his execution which took place under the emperor Nero. However, some parts of the letter suggest that he is not too far away from Philippi and that com-munication between him and the church there is not too diffi-cult. This has led others to believe that it may have written dur-ing an imprisonment in Ephesus of which no mention is made in the Acts of the Apostles. Whatever the exact background, it is clear Paul's future is uncertain and he communicates his dilemma in moving and personal terms to these people with whom he clearly has a very warm relationship. His love for Christ means that death is nothing to fear – quite the opposite, it would bring him to his Lord. On the other hand, he is aware that he has much work to do in proclaiming the gospel and so he does not know

what he should choose. His advice to the community is that they should live in a way which will not do harm to the good news which he preaches. In other words, they must avoid scandal which was very damaging to the early church, as it gave its enemies ammunition to use against it.

*Gospel: Matthew 21:1-16*
Here we find yet another parable of Jesus that is unique to this gospel, and once again the Jewish background to Matthew's community offers a key to understanding it. Parables usually have some sort of sting in the tail which demands reflection because on the surface the story makes no sense, and that is very clear in this account of the landowner's treatment of his workers. On one level it offends us because it appears to say that employers can treat their workers whatever way they like. Or on a religious level it might suggest that God can treat us whatever way he likes. But that too conjures up a very unsatisfactory picture of God. If we bear in mind that the community mostly consisting of Jewish Christians is now welcoming Gentiles into their number it gives us a context for understanding. It would be normal for the Jews to consider their Gentile neighbours as morally inferior since they practised paganism and ignored the demands of the Law of Moses. Now they come to Christ and are to be treated as equals. Surely this is too much to ask. Jesus' point is this and it applies to Christians now as well as then: the generous love of God is freely given and not earned.

*Reflection*
'Life to me, of course, is Christ.' These remarkable words would be an impressive testimony to the faith of any Christian, but when we consider they were written by Paul who had been such a zealous persecutor of the church then they are all the more amazing. They testify to the power of God's grace to bring about change in all of us and, as we are told in the first reading, we do well not to try and put limits on the ways in which God can work in our lives and the good he can do through us. We are challenged today to beware of harbouring an attitude like the workers in the vineyard. Let us give thanks for God's grace

freely poured out to everyone, even those we might consider un-deserving.

## The Twenty-sixth Sunday in Ordinary Time

*First Reading: Ezekiel 18:25-28*
We return to Ezekiel for our first reading today. However, this extract is taken from a different section of the book than the text from a few weeks ago. It deals with an important development in the way that the Israelites viewed God's dealing with sinners. In their earlier history it was thought that the sins of the parents would be visited upon the children for successive generations (Ex 43:7-8). Now, at this time of national crisis (the Babylonian exile), the prophet tells his contemporaries they must rethink their traditional ideas. Some of them are hiding behind the tradi-tion in order to say this calamity has come upon them because of the sins of their forbears. Ezekiel says it is not so! It is time for each individual to accept responsibility for his or her own wrongdoing and also to recognise the need for his or her own repentance. The prophet is affirming that God deals with them as free and responsible persons who will be held to account for their actions. As always for the great prophetic figures of the Old Testament, what is at stake here is a matter of life and death. It is only through fidelity to the covenant that they are really alive.

*Second Reading: Philippians 2:1-11*
We do not know much of what the exact situation was for the Christians in Philippi. But they would seem to be threatened with some disunity and so, as we have already seen, Paul feels the need to remind them to avoid doing anything which would dishonour the gospel message. In today's passage he continues on the theme of how they should behave; only now he is a little more specific. He calls on them to allow the reality of their life in Christ and the presence of the Spirit to bind them together in unity. In this way they will overcome whatever divisions threat-en them and not be competitive or arrogant. Their lives will be characterised by the humility that lies at the heart of Jesus' own mission. At this point Paul makes use of an early Christian

hymn which celebrates the self emptying love of Christ which brought him from the highest heavens to an ignominious death on the cross and then to the resurrection and a share in his Father's glory. This hymn was probably familiar to the community from their liturgy and in using it Paul is reminding them of the day to day consequences of the truths they acknowledge in prayer.

*Gospel: Matthew 21:28-32*
As we draw near to the end of his public ministry in Jerusalem, the conflict and tension between Jesus and the authorities increase and this is the background to the gospels over the next few weeks. This parable of the two sons is spoken to the chief priests and the elders, and interestingly the parable of the Prodigal Son in Luke 15 which is making the same point, has a similar audience. In Matthew's story the second son who says yes but does not do what is asked of him represents the authorities and is somewhat like the older brother in the Prodigal Son. God as portrayed here does not want mere external observance, or obedience from a sense of duty. The elders and chief priests fail to grasp that behind the law lies God's saving will for all people. Jesus drives this point home when he tells them that the tax collectors and prostitutes are making their way into the Kingdom of God before them.

*Reflection*
The readings today are an invitation to really make our own the faith that we profess. As with the people at the time of Ezekiel, we too sometimes like to make excuses for ourselves. We point to others' failings or to lack of good example to account for our own lack lustre commitment. Yet our faith is not in anyone else but Christ who emptied himself to become the way we are so that he might lead us to God. If we believe in him then we too must empty ourselves of everything that would keep us from being true to him. In the gospel today, Jesus is warning us rather bluntly not be to all talk when it comes to the practice of the faith, convincing ourselves that we are doing what God wants when it is not the case at all.

## THE TWENTY-SEVENTH SUNDAY IN ORDINARY TIME

*The First Reading: Isaiah 5:1-7*
These verses offer us a parable and its interpretation and they highlight in a moving and dramatic fashion the situation that existed during the life of the prophet who preached in Jerusalem for a period of some forty years beginning around 742BC.

The parable is presented as a song which tells of a vinedresser's love for and commitment to his vineyard which he had built up from nothing in the hope that it would yield a harvest of rich fruit. However, despite his best efforts it only gave him sour grapes. The prophet then turns to his audience and reveals the true meaning of his song. Israel is the vine and Yahweh the Lord is the vinedresser. As his chosen people they have received all that they needed to be faithful to the covenant but even so they have not lived as the people of God. From them he had looked for justice and integrity but all that he received was bloodshed and the cry of distress. This is a searing indictment of the social injustice which characterised their society and which was a betrayal of their unique relationship with God.

*Second Reading: Philippians 4:6-9*
This reading is taken from the last chapter of Philippians and, as we have come to expect towards the end of a letter, Paul's concern is to encourage the members of the community and to give them practical advice. The advice given is a consequence of the fact that Christ is with them. Because of this certainty there is no need to worry, but if there is anything they need they should turn to God in prayer. Interestingly Paul does not say that their every request will be granted, rather he emphasises that through prayer they will come to an awareness of God's peace and this in turn will see them through. It will help them to keep their focus on Christ Jesus and allow them to live their lives in a manner worthy of their Christian calling.

*Gospel: Matthew 21:33-43*
Following on from the critique of the authorities in last Sunday's gospel, we have another incident in which a parable serves to show up the hard-heartedness of the leaders. This time the im-

agery for the parable comes from the Old Testament traditions that liken Israel to a vineyard, planted and protected by God. The important aspect of the parable is the attitude to the harvest. In the Isaiah reading today the problem was the sour grapes but now it shifts to the idea that the tenants think that are the owners and they should decide what to do with the harvest. In essence, they have not only forgotten what they owe to God but are cutting themselves off from him. Jesus rebukes them for this and warns that the vineyard will be taken from them and given to those who will deliver its fruit in due season. The leaders' rejection of Jesus prepares the way for the events of Holy Week. Ironically, by plotting to be rid of him, they are opening up the way for the vineyard to be shared by all.

*Reflection*
As with the parable of the two sons, the temptation with this story is to read it as a condemnation of another people in another time. But that is not why it is proclaimed in our Sunday Eucharist. When we assemble as a community we are reminded that it is the risen Lord who calls us together. He blesses us with forgiveness and strengthens us through the Eucharist, yet he is also asking for the fruits of Christian living. Are we caring for the weak among us? Are we working for reconciliation or are we guilty of hypocrisy? This Sunday, let us look at the vineyard that we have been given and ask ourselves 'Are we good tenants?'

THE TWENTY-EIGHTH SUNDAY IN ORDINARY TIME

*First Reading: Isaiah 25:6-10*
The rich symbolism of this reading is worth pondering for it conveys a very joyful image of the faithful generosity of God. The context for the prophecy is the oppression which has been experienced by the inhabitants of Jerusalem as a result of the expansion of the Assyrian empire. The entire world is under the control of this ruthless system and the people feel abandoned by their God. Into this situation of sadness and want, the prophet speaks God's word of hope and promise. The reversal of their fortunes is symbolised by a banquet which God himself will prepare on Mount Zion (i.e. Jerusalem). Famine and mourning will

give way to rejoicing and celebration as the Lord wipes away their tears. The people will understand that they have not waited in vain. In Hebrew the same word is used for 'to wait' and 'to hope' and towards the end of our reading we can see that the people's waiting for God to act is the same as hoping in him. It is grounded in the certainty that their God cannot forget them.

### Second Reading: Philippians 4:12-14, 19-20

Remembering that Paul wrote to the Philippians from prison will help us to understand his concluding remarks which are to be found in this reading. The Christian community in Philippi had sent provisions to Paul in jail and he wishes to thank them for their concern. Their generosity to him gives him the opportunity to reflect on the fact that his work for the gospel has led him into all kinds of situations. He has learned through all his experiences, whether good or bad, to depend on the grace of God who gives him the strength he needs for every situation. In saying this he is not making little of their kindness to him, indeed the knowledge of their concern for him in prison is a source of consolation to him and he is sure that God will bless them for their goodness to him.

### Gospel: Matthew 22:1-14

Once again we are presented with a parable with a sting in the tail that leaves us wondering what Jesus is trying to tell us. And once again we will be helped in our efforts to understand it if we remember Matthew's context: a Jewish Christian community which is also in the process of welcoming Gentiles. In the Old Testament marriage is used as a symbol of the covenant between God and his people and the banquet, as in today's first reading, is a symbol of God's generous love. In the parable, the three groups invited represent the stages of the history of salvation. The first group is the people of the Old Testament who rejected the prophets. The second group is the leaders at the time of Jesus who reject him, and the third are the Gentiles of Matthew's time. The incident over the wedding garment is addressed to them. It means that we cannot just turn up at the feast, we are called to repentance, to a new way of living. In the early church, being baptised was likened to putting on Christ, a new garment (Col 3:12-15).

*Reflection*
'There is no such thing as a free lunch' or so the saying goes. The underlying thought here is that you get nothing for nothing and it is, no doubt, an accurate reflection of many people's experience. However, when the prophet Isaiah was looking for a way to show his downtrodden contemporaries just what their God was really like, he chose the image of the free sumptuous banquet. Like us, they had been so drawn into the ways of the world that they had forgotten the unparalleled generosity of their God. Like them, we need to turn around and sit at God's table and let him serve. We also need to make a connection between accepting this generosity of God and witnessing to it in our own lives. So let's turn up properly dressed!

## The Twenty-ninth Sunday in Ordinary Time

*First Reading: Isaiah 45:1, 4-6*
Without some awareness of the background, it would be very difficult to know what this reading is about. The part of the book from which it comes (chapters 40-55) is known as Second Isaiah. It dates from a period several hundred years after the death of the prophet Isaiah and the author of this section of the book is unknown. What is known, however, is that he was writing at the time when the Jews, who had been exiled to Babylon, were being told by Cyrus, the king of Persia who had destroyed the Babylonians, that they could go back home to Jerusalem. The writing in these chapters is full of hope and joy as the people look forward to their return. It also contains a very universal perspective and for the first time among the Israelites we see a clear statement that their God, Yahweh, is the only God and that everything is subject to his will and that all history is under his control. Thus when we read that God calls Cyrus 'his anointed' it comes as a shock, for this is the same as saying to this foreign king 'you are my messiah'. Until this time it would have been thought that there were many gods competing for control. The Israelites saw Yahweh as the God of their territory, while other nations had their gods. Now, in a huge step forward, the prophet recognises that even the rise of Cyrus as king of Persia is Yahweh's work. Even though he does not know it, he is doing

God's work in letting the Israelites go home. The truth is now dawning that Yahweh is not only Lord in Israel but is the only God under heaven.

*Second Reading: 1 Thessalonians 1:1-5*
This is probably the earliest writing in the New Testament having been sent by Paul to the Christians in Thessalonica around AD51. At that time he was in Corinth and had heard from Timothy a very good report about how things were going in the community, so he wrote to them a word of encouragement and congratulations. We can get some idea of the background by reading Acts 17:1-18:11. The opening of the letter follows the pattern of the other New Testament epistles, introducing Paul and those who are with him and moving on to an expression of thanksgiving for all the blessings they have received. It is clear from these few verses that Paul is delighted with how things are going in this young church. They are showing their faith by their actions and are driven in all that they do by the power of the Holy Spirit. We might remember from earlier in the year how the readings from 1 Corinthians showed that community in quite a different light. It is noteworthy how Paul emphasises the role of the Father, the Son and the Spirit in all authentic Christian living.

*Gospel: Matthew 22:15-21*
Today's gospel shows the cobbling together of an unholy alliance in an effort to trap Jesus. The Pharisees had little in common with the Herodians but both saw that his preaching of the kingdom was a threat to their worldviews, whether religious or political. The Herodians were supporter of King Herod Antipas, a puppet king allowed to rule by the Romans; the Pharisees, on the other hand, opposed Roman rule and the paying of tax to the emperor. By means of their question they hope to either discredit Jesus with the Jews, by showing him as a collaborator, or to land him in trouble with the Romans for encouraging the withholding of tax. Jesus' answer highlights their hypocrisy. The coin he is given has on it an image of the emperor and an inscription calling him the son of the deified Augustus, and with a simple reply Jesus avoids their trap. If you use Caesar's coinage for

your business then you owe him tax but remember God must always have first claim on your hearts.

*Reflection*
It is sometimes said that religion and politics don't mix, but it is very often hard to separate them. They are both concerned with how we live our lives though from different perspectives, and today's gospel and first reading help to illustrate the difference. As Christians we are not called to live in ivory towers detached from the world and its problems. Rather we are to respond to the world with a kingdom perspective, in other words, we are asked to do what Jesus did. Our politics must always be informed by the vision Jesus offers us of a world in which God cares for everyone.

THE THIRTIETH SUNDAY IN ORDINARY TIME

*First Reading: Exodus 22: 20-26*
The Book of Exodus tells how Moses led the Israelites from slavery in Egypt out to Mount Sinai where they entered into a covenant with their liberating God. On Sinai the stipulations of the covenant are given and we know these through the summary contained in the Ten Commandments. However, in this reading we see some of the details of the Law of Moses that highlight the relationship between the nature of God and the way he wants his people to live. Yahweh had acted to save the Israelites because they were downtrodden and oppressed, so now as his people they must never oppress the weaker or more vulnerable members of their society. To do so would be to completely fail to recognise what God had done for them. God does not make laws just because he can – rather God gives them laws that reflect who he is and his passion for justice and peace.

*Second Reading: 1 Thessalonians 1:5-10*
The positive tone of the opening of this letter continues with Paul praising the new converts for their wholehearted engagement with their new life in Christ. He alludes to the fact that this was not easy for them but now the word about them has spread throughout the Christian communities not only in Greece but

further afield and is a source of joy for the whole church. The change they have undergone is a remarkable one since as, pagans, they would have been influenced by a very superficial and superstitious worldview. Now in welcoming Christ and living by his Spirit they have taken a stand against that and this would set them apart from their fellow citizens and no doubt attract negative comment and some persecution. Paul refers to his belief that the second coming of Christ and final judgement would be soon.

## Gospel: Matthew 22:34-40

The opponents of Jesus are still lining up to challenge him and, having just dealt with the Sadduccees before this, the Pharisees now decide to try and engage in some theological word play. The question they put to him is important but the reason for doing it is not so much to know the truth but to try and engage in debates that would show Jesus as belonging to one camp or another. In his answer, Jesus gets quickly to the heart of the matter by reminding them of what they already know. The God they serve is a God of love so they must love God and their neighbour. These two sides of their life of faith cannot be separated and in fact they sum up the entire biblical story.

## Reflection

Knowing the right answer does not always mean that we will do the right thing and today's gospel shows how true that is. It is relatively easy to talk about religion and even to feel very passionate about it. However, that is no guarantee that we will be living the kind of life God wants from us. Loving God means loving your neighbour. Not just the deserving neigbour or the helpful neighbour or the Christian neighbour. God is presenting himself to us in many disguises and in our hurry to go to Mass we could be ignoring him in lots of different ways.

### The Thirty-first Sunday in Ordinary Time

*First Reading: Malachi 1:14-2:2, 8-10*
The prophet Malachi (the name means 'my messenger') preached around 450BC and his message is a hard-hitting one, especially for the priests. After the return from exile and the rebuilding of the temple in 520BC, many people were hopeful of a great religious renewal but, with the passage of time, these hopes were dashed. In this reading, the prophet denounces the priests for their failure to properly instruct the people and for their half-hearted service to the Lord. He warns them that even the pagan nations worship in a way which is more acceptable. Finally, he reminds them that God is their Father, the one who created them all and so they should treat one another accordingly as equals and not abuse their position.

*Second Reading: 1 Thessalonians 2:7-9, 13*
The positive note that was struck at the beginning of the letter continues and in this section Paul is recalling the depth of his concern, and that of his assistants, as they worked among the new converts in Thessalonica. Their mission gave them a sense of protective care towards the community, to such an extent that they were totally drawn into sharing their whole lives with them. It was not simply a matter of preaching the gospel but of working alongside them so that they could pay their own way. However, it was very much a labour of love because the Thessalonians understood very quickly the importance of the message they were hearing. This was not just another philosophy but indeed God's powerful word at work among them.

*Gospel: Matthew 23:1-12*
The direct confrontations with Jesus' opponents have come to an end and now he addresses his words to the crowds and his disciple. However, there can be no doubt that his message is derived from his experience of the religious and political leaders of his time. These verses contain a stinging attack on the hypocrisy of the Pharisees who exploit their place in society to win people's approval but who in fact do nothing to help anyone.

The phylacteries Jesus refers to are the little wooden boxes containing some words of the Torah of Moses which were tied to the head and left forearm in a literal interpretation of Deuteronomy 11:18. This type of self-aggrandisement is the exact opposite of what the followers of Jesus should aspire to. They are all brothers and sisters under their one Father and their only model of leadership is that of service as exemplified by Jesus himself.

*Reflection*
It is very easy to become tired, to slip into laxity especially when things are fine. It is very likely that the priests at the time of Malachi thought they were doing a grand job now that the temple was rebuilt and sacrifices were taking place. The harshness of the prophet's criticisms probably hurt them or caused deep resentment, and no doubt this would have been true of Jesus' words as well. The fact is, however, that sometimes hard words need to be said. Sometimes we in the church can hear the words of the gospel as though they are intended for somebody else, and that they do not apply to us. That is a fatal error and leads to the kind of complacency that Jesus so vigourously rejects.

THE THIRTY-SECOND WEEK IN ORDINARY TIME

*First Reading: Wisdom 6:12-16*
The Book of Wisdom is probably the latest book in the Old Testament, being written only some 60 years before the birth of Jesus. It was written in Greek unlike most of the Old Testament, which was written in Hebrew, and the reason for this is quite simple. It was intended for well-educated, Greek-speaking Jews who lived in Alexandria. Their faith was under threat from the culture in which they were living which valued philosophy very highly and tended to downplay the importance of the Law of Moses and the historical events which were so central to Jewish faith. The author reminds his readers of the importance of the search for wisdom in their own tradition and attempts to show how their religion is very relevant to the world in which they are living. The verses we read today take up a theme that is found elsewhere in the Old Testament and that is the personification of wisdom (cf Proverbs 8, and Sirach 24). In other words wisdom,

which is a gift of God, is presented as a woman who seeks to guide those who search for her along the right path. This reading encourages those who look for wisdom to continue with their search and to be vigilant, for their efforts will not be in vain.

*Second Reading: 1 Thessalonians 4:13-18*
In this section of the letter, Paul is addressing a very specific problem which is worrying some of the community and it concerns the death of their loved ones. Since they believe that Jesus is going to return again soon some people are wondering about those who have already died. What will happen to them, will they not share in the glory of heaven in the same way as those who are alive when Christ comes? Paul (who at this time also believes that the end is near) immediately puts their minds at rest by insisting that those who are alive at the time of Christ's coming will have no advantage over those who have already died. He then goes on to describe the second coming using apocalyptic language. Some fundamentalists take this description literally and make much use of this passage in their efforts to say when and how the world will end. However, the central message here concerns the fact that even though we do not know when the world will end, we may be sure that all those who have believed in Jesus will share in the reward of eternal life.

*Gospel: Matthew 25:1-13*
For the the last three Sundays of Year A, the gospel readings will be parables taken from taken from Matthew 25. They all look forward to the end time but with an eye very much on the present. As the liturgical year draws to a close, we are asked to be aware that we believe that Christ will come again and that our attitude to now is to be informed by that understanding. In the parable for today, the story of the ten bridesmaids, the element of surprise or shock is present again as it seems that selfish behaviour is commended. That cannot be the case, so what is the point of the story? The background may be the custom whereby the bridesmaids accompanied the groom to the bride's house after he had successfully negotiated the dowry with the bride's father. In our story, there is an unexplained delay which means that the foolish bridesmaids will be shown up for their lack of

preparedness. When the groom arrives at midnight it is time for the festivities to begin, but only those wise bridesmaids with oil in their lamps can participate fully. The point of the story is that we must strive to be wise, i.e. ready for the sudden and sometimes unforeseen demands of our Christian living. It is easy to fall into a rut, to be caught up in the day to day things and to forget the bigger picture. Christ reveals himself to us in ways and at times we do not expect so he call us to be vigilant.

*Reflection*
Wisdom is not a course we are likely to see in a school or university curriculum, yet in our time there is great interest in personal development and various paths to wholeness and happiness. The trouble with much of this material is that it is totally self-obsessed and in this way it contrasts with the wisdom spoken of in the Bible. It brings the seeker out of him or herself towards the ultimate truth which can only be found in God. That is why Jesus is often described in terms of wisdom, and if our search for him is authentic then we will come to true knowledge of ourselves and to the peace and contentment that only God can give.

### THE THIRTY-THIRD SUNDAY IN ORDINARY TIME

*First Reading: Proverbs 31:10-13, 30-31*
The Book of Proverbs is a collection of wisdom sayings and reflections, which extends back several hundred years over the history of Israel. Unlike the other books of the Bible, it does not concern itself with the actions of God in the past, nor indeed the Law in the present. Rather it deals with the day to day experience of life and offers the collective wisdom of generations of wise men. That it was the men who were deliberating on these issues is clear from today's reading, which focuses on the virtues of the perfect wife. A more balanced text would also give us some thoughts on the perfect husband but Israel was a patriarchal society and so there is no such writing. However, there is a value in reflecting on this description, for the important virtues which are emphasised here are applicable to everyone. Her talents are used for the good of others and she is particularly concerned with the plight of the poor. The sentiments of the second

last verse may also be applied to either sex: 'Charm is deceitful, and beauty empty; the person who is wise is the one to praise.'

*Second Reading: 1 Thessalonians 5:1-6*
As we noted the previous Sunday, the question of the Second Coming of Jesus was something which exercised the minds of many early Christians. Now, in the closing verses of this letter, Paul moves to put an end to fruitless speculation about the exact timing of this event. For him, the essential point is that Christians must always try to live according to the gospel and its values. We cannot predict the end for it will come upon us at a time we do not expect. However, it is not as though we must live in fear of the end, like someone afraid of the dark. On the contrary, because of Jesus we are now children of the light and so we need only concern ourselves with being true to him.

*Gospel: Matthew 25:14-30*
The focus on the future remains as we come to the second last Sunday of the liturgical year, and once again Jesus uses the idea of the kingdom in a way which shows it is as much a way of living as it is our final destiny. In the Parable of the Talents a man leaves his servants certain sums of money as he heads away on a long journey. The idea is that they should use the money wisely so that the master gets a good return for his investment. The term 'talent' refers to the largest unit of currency of the time and is the equivalent of about a quarter of a million euro today. Two of the servants manage to double the money while the third more or less opts out by simply hiding it in the ground. On the master's return, he commends the first two servants warmly for their action. While we might expect him to be disappointed with the third what we get is a tirade as he turns on this hapless individual calling him wicked, lazy and 'good for nothing'. The by now familiar pattern of the shock aspect of the parable confronts us again. Jesus wants us to realise that the kingdom is about using our talents, not hiding them. It is about being out there and using our God-given gifts to promote the kingdom that Jesus has proclaimed.

*Reflection*
How often do we hear phrases like 'I am a good person. I do no-one any harm.' This is the thinking that Jesus challenges today. It is a negative response to our calling which in the parable is likened to an adventure that involves taking risks. As the year comes to an end, perhaps we could ask ourselves in what way have we used our gifts for the sake of the kingdom? Like Paul's Christians we are still looking forward to the end and the second coming, and no doubt Paul and his contemporaries would be amazed to discover that even after 2000 years Christ had still not come again. However, if he were here now he would still be giving the same advice to those who are trying to predict the end and to those who are worried about it. Maybe it would read like this: 'Try to live every day as if it were your last, using your gifts and living life to the full in the sure knowledge that you are infinitely loved by your eternal Father.'

THE FEAST OF CHRIST THE KING

*First Reading: Ezekiel 34:11-12, 15-17*
The idea that God alone is king in Israel extends far back to the times before there was a monarchy. Later on, after the introduction of dynastic rule with King David (1000BC) the monarch was there as a representative of God and was to care for the flock entrusted to him as a shepherd cares for his sheep (2 Sam 7:8). The context for the verses we read today is the plight of the people of Israel who have been forced into exile in Babylon. In a strong condemnation of their kings and leaders, the prophet highlights their failures as those of self-serving shepherds who are only concerned for their own well-being and who have ignored the needs of their flock. All of chapter 34 is given over to a treatment of this imagery and the contrast between their leaders and their God. Yahweh, who is the only real king in Israel, will from now on shepherd the flock himself. He will gather the scattered people and lead them from their experience of mist and darkness to a safe pasture where they may rest. Those who have been injured will be healed and the weak shall be made strong. This is the exercise of true leadership and authority as envisaged in the covenant.

*Second Reading: 1 Corinthians 15:20-26, 28*
Chapter 15 of 1 Corinthians is given over to Paul's teaching on the resurrection. He devoted time to it because some in the community had questioned whether or not Christ truly did rise. In treating of this topic, Paul speaks not only about the historical fact of the resurrection but also about its consequences, and in the verses we read today the resurrection of Jesus is seen as the starting point for the move towards the final resurrection of all the dead. Paul's point is that at the end of time Christ will exercise fully and completely the power to bring all people to life, a power symbolised and anticipated in his own resurrection from the dead.

*Gospel: Matthew 25:31-46*
The last act of Jesus' public ministry in Matthew's gospel is to tell a parable in which the last judgement is described. We should remember this is a story and not a prediction but as with all the parables it is aimed at making us stop and think. Two sets of people are surprised in this story and both express their amazement with the same question: 'But when Lord did we see you in need?' One group, the righteous are amazed to find that they have been serving the Lord when they helped the poor and needy. Equally, the others are horrified to discover that every time they ignored the poor and needy they were ignoring their Lord. If we have been paying close attention to Matthew's gospel this year, this parable will not come as surprise because time and again Jesus in his proclamation of the kingdom has appealed for people to be authentic in the living of their faith, in other words to make their deeds match their words. We must actively do the will of the Father and be loving as he is loving.

*Reflection*
The readings for the feast we celebrate today are well chosen because they invite us to reflect on what kind of ruler Jesus is. The model given in Ezekiel is the model of the Good Shepherd, whose only concern is the well being of those entrusted to him. With Paul we come to understand that the power Christ exercises is the power to give life and these are the two characteristics which define Jesus' ministry among us. The gospel for today highlights the fact that as followers of Christ the King we will be judged on the extent to

which our actions are life-giving, especially for those in need. We have a share in his royal authority, that is, we too are called to serve.